MANDALA

MANDALA

Creating an Authentic Spiritual Path

An InterSpiritual Process

EDWARD W. BASTIAN

The Spiritual Paths Series

Albion
Andalus
Boulder, Colorado
2014

"The old shall be renewed,
and the new shall be made holy."
— Rabbi Avraham Yitzhak Kook

Albion-Andalus Inc.
P. O. Box 19852
Boulder, CO 80308
www.albionandalus.com

Design and composition by Albion-Andalus Inc.

Cover design by Sari Wisenthal-Shore.

Watercolor image of the "Spiritual Paths Mandala" on the cover
envisioned by Edward W. Bastian and painted by Sharon Wells.

Photos of Edward W. Bastian by Charles Abbott and Michael
Stinson

Manufactured in the United States of America

ISBN-13: 978-0692242698 (Albion-Andalus Books)
ISBN-10: 0692242694

To the spirit of my sister Marianne,
A natural-born bodhisattva
Who exemplified a life of unbounded
Love, kindness, caring, generosity and humor.

CONTENTS

PART III
YOUR SPIRITUAL PROFILE

ACKNOWLEDGMENTS

THE SCOPE OF THIS WORK broadened and deepened my relationship with many extraordinary teachers, students, friends and family members. I will simply mention their names here without being specific as to why. Sadly, I will have forgotten some significant names that later editions will try to include. Please forgive me if yours is one of these.

I am indebted to living examples of my mentors and teachers, especially His Holiness the Dalai Lama, Geshe Lhundup Sopa, Father Thomas Keating, and Rabbi Zalman Schachter-Shalomi. I wish to thank the team of core teachers for the Spiritual Paths Foundation with whom I worked and developed the Mandala Process since 2002: Swami Atmarupananda, Sheikh Kabir and Sheikha Camille Helminski, Rabbi Rami Shapiro, and Rev. Cynthia Bourgeault.

I am deeply grateful to Rev. Gregg Anderson and the Aspen Chapel for providing the Aspen home for Spiritual Paths Foundation and our Aspen-based board of directors, including: Jay Hughes, Suzanne Farver, John Bennett, Lexie Potamkin, John Sarpa, and Mike Stranahan. I am extremely grateful to Juliet Spohn Twomey and La Casa de Maria for providing encouragement and a Santa Barbara home for this work. I deeply appreciate my Santa Barbara friends and supporters, including: John Cleese, Dr. Michael Kearney, Dr. Radhule Weininger, Harvey and Patsy Bottleson, George Haynes, Bay Hallowell, Christiane Schlumberger, Dr. Tony Alina and Robbie Bosnak.

I wish to thank my fellow executive committee members of the Interfaith Initiative and ECOFaith of Santa Barbara, including: Ivor John, Prof. Kathleen Moore, Rev. Doug Miller, Cantor Mark Childs. I am especially grateful to Bishop Bill Swing and my fellow members of the environmental cooperation circle and Trustees on the Global Council of the United Religions Initiative.

My deep thanks to teaching colleagues Lauren Van Ham, Dean

of the Chaplaincy Institute, Juliet Rhode Brown, Dean of the PsyD program at Antioch Universisty, Santa Barbara and Rev. Diane Berke and Kurt Johnson of One Spirit Interfaith Seminary.

My deep gratitude to Spiritual Paths teachers, colleagues and supporters, including: Reverend Lauren Artress, Rabbi Ozer Bergman, Mother Tessa Bielecki, Bikkhu Bodhi, Joan Borysenko, Cynthia Brix, Mary Ann Brussat, Loya Cespooch, Nancy Belle Coe, Sister Brahmaprana, Ken Cohen, Katherine and Roger Collis, Kathy Corcoran, Anita Daniel, Father David Denny, Laura Dixon, Geshe Lobsang Donyo, Lama Palden Drolma, Gordon Dveirin, Mollie Favour, Rob Gabriel, Gelek Rinpoche, Stephanie Glatt, John Allen Grimes, Roshi Joan Halifax, Rabbi Brad Hirschfield, Sister Jose Hobday, Judy Hyde, Pir Zia Inayat-Khan, Don "Four Arrows" Jacobs, Reverend Alan Jones, Will Keepin, Chief Oren Lyons, Yogi Nataraja Kallio, Rabbi Miles Krassen, Reverend Master Khoten, Acharya Judy Lief, Amitai Zachary Malone, Robert McDermott, Dena Merriam, Brad Miller, Sheikh Muhammad Jamal al-Jerrahi (Gregory Blann), Enrico and Nadia Natali, Rabbi Leah Novick, Susan Pierce, Reverend Tenzin Priyadarshi, Margot and Tom Pritzker, Lynda Rae, Imam Feisal Abdul Rauf, Jonathan and Diana Rose, Rabbi Jeff Roth, Sharon Salzburg, Barbara Sargent, Swami Sarvadevananda, Rabbi Arthur Gross Schaefer, Marilyn Schlitz, Grace Alvarez Sesma, Acharya Judith Simmer-Brown, Ajahn Sona, Tina Staley, Tekaronianeken Jake Swamp, Geshe Lobsang Tenzin, Ani Tenzin Kacho, Pravrajika Vrajaprana, Dr. B. Alan Wallace, Judy Whetstine and Paula Zurcher.

I am also grateful to all those who have studied InterSpiritual Meditation and the Spiritual Paths Mandala Process with me, for they have helped to clarify and refine the ideas and practices described herein.

I offer deep thanks to Carol Pearson for her advice and encouragement on the creation of the Spiritual Styles Profiling Tool, Catherine Wyler and Stella Bonnie for editing and comments on the manuscript. Sharon Wells for artistically helping me create the Spiritual Paths Mandala, and Netanel Miles-Yépez for editing and publishing my books over the years.

I send my eternal gratitude to my brother Ken for exhorting me to complete this work over 25 years ago. To my sister Marianne who exemplified a life of compassion, caring and kindness. My eternal love to family members, especially, Jonathan Bastian,

Acknowledgments

Alexandra and Nulty White, Paul Keeley, Lesley Bastian, Anna Souza, Mariana Souza, Edie Irons, Ann and Ken Bastian, and to all my other relatives past, present and future. I send my everlasting love and gratitude for the birth of my grandson, Harlan Francis White, and his offspring who may come across these words far into the future.

— E.W.B.

PREFACE

WITH THE DAWN of a new millennium, the circumstances have never been better for us to reclaim our spiritual destinies. Cultural diversity, the Internet, the proliferation of books and personal mobility have all opened up new opportunities to explore the world's spiritual traditions. We no longer need to rely exclusively on local religious institutions and teachers to guide us on our personal paths, especially if their methods and doctrines are not satisfying. But if we choose to take advantage of these new opportunities, we must also begin to take more personal responsibility. We can no longer be comforted by the idea that our spiritual destinies are in someone else's hands, beyond our ability to control. Electing to explore a personal spiritual path implies a willingness to tackle the truly profound and difficult challenges of life 'head on'—to take the intrepid inner journey, to wander into the unexplored crevasses of human consciousness and discover truths about ourselves that have long been hidden.

Taking this kind of personal responsibility requires us to draw deeply on our own experiences and innate spiritual abilities, building on the insights, methods and examples that have been handed down to us by the world's great religions. Unfortunately, the spiritual treasures left us by the founders and saints of different religious paths, especially those which lead to primary experiences, have often been hidden behind a multitude of institutional veils. These façades, constructed by those who were obsessed with institutional survival and domination, often prevented access to the original spiritual wealth upon which these institutions were founded.

This book represents an attempt to reverse this trend. It suggests a methodology for constructing and cultivating a personal spiritual path from the world's collective spiritual wisdom, utilizing our own preferences and learning styles to find the answers to our most profound questions. That is to say, it provides the process, not the answers; those we must find ourselves. Thus, it should be thought of as a self-initiated educational program for cultivating what emerges from within, rather than beginning with established religious dogmas and institutions to which we must conform and fit ourselves. It is instead a process that we can undertake on our own and which we can use as a tool for helping ourselves and others.

We begin the process by first identifying our own inherent spiritual learning style, which in turn provides us with a foundation for answering our spiritual questions, finding teachers and practices and formulating our own spiritual path. The process then continues with a systematic study of the knowledge and practices within one or more of the spiritual traditions that will support the development of that path.

However, in this very personal process of study, we cannot avoid the challenge and benefit of having good, reliable teachers, people who can authentically represent and transmit spiritual knowledge and practices from their own traditions. This might lead to deep immersion within a single tradition with a qualified teacher who honors our personal styles of learning. Therefore, a balance must be found between critical thinking, intuitive experience, and well-placed respect, faith and devotion toward authentic spiritual teachers and teachings. This need for discernment also extends to our integration of the wisdom from secular traditions such as science, psychology, mythology and philosophy. Here, a qualified mentor can also help us avoid the pitfalls of misinterpreting or misappropriating the beliefs and practices of various traditions as we integrate them into our personal spiritual path.

In order to help you relate to and utilize this process, I have included stories from my own life—how I arrived at this method and how I apply it in my own study and practice of Buddhism. Whether you seek to create your own personal path within a single tradition, or from among a variety of traditions, I would suggest that you begin a journal organized around the categories described in this book wherein you can collect the truths and practices that define your own inner path and reflect on your own process.

Work with the Spiritual Paths Mandala is further deepened through an engagement with the seven steps of InterSpiritual Meditation (ISM). This meditative and contemplative process is designed to be customized by each individual according to their own spiritual style and questions. It is a method for gaining deep insight and direct experience into the nature and purpose of our lives. Together, the Mandala and ISM help us to develop a solid and sustainable inner foundation for integrating and bringing our deepest insights and values into the world.*

— EDWARD W. BASTIAN

---

* On-line and in-person classes and individual mentoring are offered on the "Mandala Process" and on InterSpiritual Meditation. In addition, these are the core subjects for a certificate training program in InterSpiritual Mentoring. For more information on these offerings, please visit www.spiritualpaths.net.

INTRODUCTION

BACK IN 1970, I was privileged to be working with the legendary Lowell Thomas in India on a documentary which included a lengthy interview with His Holiness, the 14th Dalai Lama. After the filming was completed, I was granted a number of private interviews with His Holiness, during which, he instructed me for the first time in the central concepts of Buddhism.

During these sessions, I explained to him how young Americans like myself were determined to change the world. I told him that, although there were many things about America we appreciated, we were vehemently against the war in Viet Nam and determined to remake America into a truly egalitarian force for peace in the world. We wanted to protect the environment and overturn the corrupt power structures, governed by greed and racism. We wanted to celebrate America's ethnic and racial diversity and sought equality for women in all aspects of American society. I also told him that we saw how many religious institutions were connected to a corrupt power structure. One that supported the status quo and colluded with a political and economic elite to repress our desires to be liberated from an unjust system. At the same time, I also quizzed him intensely about Buddhism. I told him how disillusioned I had become with my own culture and religion, and how I admired him for being at once a spiritual and political leader.

He then gave me my first oral teachings on the Buddhist concepts of impermanence, interdependence, emptiness and compassion—ways of looking at reality that took me years to absorb and comprehend. He explained to me how ignorance is the source of all our miseries; it begins with a misconception about our own nature, and the nature of the reality we perceive all around us. "We are imprisoned, "he said, "by our ignorance. It is impossible to be free from the prison of suffering, or to help liberate others, without knowing both the cause and the cure for ignorance."

As an example of this impermanence and interdependence, His Holiness pointed to the chair in front of us and asked: "Where is the real chair? Is it in the legs, the seat, the back, the arms or the upholstery? Is it all of these things together? What happens when you remove its parts? Is it still a chair? You see, the word 'chair' is simply a name that we project on an interdependent structure that has no basis for its existence beyond its parts and our perception of them. So, no matter how solid or precious that chair may seem to you, there is, ultimately, no independently existing thing to be attached to."

Then he asked: "Where is the real, permanent Ed?" Is it in your body, your feelings, your senses, or your mind? Is there an Ed that doesn't change, that isn't dependent on all these constituents? Is it in your soul? Doesn't the reality of Ed change from being a baby, to a teenager, to an adult, to an old man? So, isn't it true that there is no final Ed to be attached to that chair?" Finally, he concluded: "It is this ignorant belief that we ourselves, as well the things around us, are inherently real that is the cause of our suffering."

Well, this was pretty tough medicine for a young American midwesterner, taught to identify with my body and to believe that the world was as solid and real as it appeared to my senses. Not that these views made perfect sense to me; but to challenge them seemed to throw certainty to the wind and to embrace a frightening kind of chaos. And yet, the Dalai Lama seemed to be perfectly well. He seemed sane, happy, well-balanced, and a whole lot wiser and more compassionate than the religious and political leaders I had known in America. Moreover, his way of thinking seemed more compatible with the little I had learned about modern physics and psychology than the Christian dogma I had grown up with. So I began to wonder if Buddhism, with its logical approach to life, might be something more suitable for me and my temperament.

Thinking about all these possibilities, my mind began to spin. The Dalai Lama looked at me and laughed playfully. At that point, Tenzin Geyche, His Holiness' secretary, reminded him of his next appointment. Then His Holiness told me that I could now begin my formal studies with Geshe Rabten, his so-called "junior tutor." He also invited me to return for more conversations. So began my journey on the Buddhist path.

Introduction

THE ASPEN COMMUNITY SCHOOL

After my initial studies of Buddhist meditation with Geshe Rabten, I returned to Aspen, Colorado, to start my life over on the Buddhist path. I had moved there in 1969, leaving New York City for this little mountain oasis, trading-in my Saks Fifth Avenue suits and ties for jeans and tee shirts, my cherished Greenwich Village apartment for a tent by a stream, my typewriter for a landscaping shovel, taxis and trains for a beat up GMC pickup truck. In New York, my jobs had included political organizing for Governor Rockefeller, writing for NBC News, and documentary filmmaking; but in Colorado I worked as a landscaper and tried to orient my life around simpler, more natural rhythms.

When I returned to Aspen from India, I soon fell in with a group of friends who wanted to start a new kind of school. We were all passionate about education, seeing it as the most powerful long-term change-agent in our society. We felt that American schools had adopted an industrial, assembly-line approach to education in which students were regarded as mere products to be fabricated. Education was not freeing our minds, as it should, but forcing them into conformity, and indoctrinating them for obedience to a system. It seemed that we were being trained to become mere cogs, automata in the military-industrial complex. Schools, as we saw it, were just not living up to their profound potential for helping us to become fully actualized human beings.

The chief problem was the one-size-fits-all approach to education. Students were being forced to conform to a standardized system of education that just wasn't suitable for all students. They were not seen as individuals, but as entities into which information could be systematically downloaded. Likewise, the standardized tests of this system enforced conformity, and ended up measuring our personal worth. Our self-image was predicated on our score and ranking in relation to other students. Thus, our future happiness, economic earning potential, and social status would depend on how well we scored and were measured by these tests. This seemed like a violation of our basic human rights. We were being *told* by our guidance counselors who and what we could become based on tests we took as children and teenagers. The system was shutting down our potential before we could even begin to ask our own questions or form our own opinions about what we could or should become. So we set out to create a better form of education

– XIX –

for our children.

At the same time, we were also trying to recreate ourselves. We were learning about other belief-systems and other spiritual paths: Hinduism, Buddhism, Taoism, Sufism, and Native American spirituality. In these spiritual traditions, we were inspired by what we had not found in the more conventional versions of American Christianity and Judaism with which we had grown up. We also discovered that there were more esoteric and profound versions of these traditions as well. We learned about other possibilities for spiritual liberation, opportunities to know and understand our true identities, to self-actualize the God or the infinite potential that is within us. We learned that by changing our *karma* we could control our own destinies. We learned that inner peace and wisdom was required for external peace in the world. We learned to meditate, to practice yoga and tai chi as means of creating that inner peace and harmony with nature. We learned to see ourselves as interdependent parts of an eco-system, rather than a superior species born to assert our dominion over the environment. As Bobby Dylan put it, the times were clearly "a changin'" and we took him seriously when he said, "get out of the way if you can't lend a hand." So, in Aspen, during the spring and summer of 1970, we started The Aspen Community School.

In truth, it was a small group of parents who really led the way for the new school in Aspen. Some of them had children who were somewhat hyperactive, and others who were simply not able to learn effectively with the standardized teaching methods and curriculum offered in ordinary schools. Some were artistic, some were rebels, and some were geniuses. They wanted something better for their kids, and they had the courage to strike out on their own and to create a new school. Then there were others like me, who simply joined-in, adding enthusiasm to the mix, organizing rock concerts and bake sales to raise money. We didn't expect to earn a living at this; we just wanted to be a part of something good, something that would create the kind of tangible change for which we yearned.

We all wanted to create a learning community that was truly respectful of an individual child's needs. We called the approach "child-centered." The individual student was our main focus and we tried to help the children learn according to their own unique capacities and styles. Moreover, the parents were equally involved in the educational process, not simply observers and enforcers as they are in conventional schools. As we saw it, parents and children were equal participants in the school's educational process.

Together, we read books like *Summerhill* by Alexander Neill, the works of philosophers and psychologists like John Dewey, Abraham Maslow and Carl Rogers. Several professional teachers with direct experience of this type of education were also hired. A little money was then raised, a building at the Aspen Center for Physics was donated, and about sixty kids between the ages of 5 and 13 were enrolled. A few days before the first day of classes, we all sat around our new school to plan the schedule and to determine who would teach the various classes. I remember how someone turned to me and said, "Hey Ed, what are you going to teach?"

"Teach?" I asked. "You mean you really want *me* to teach? What can *I* teach?"

"Well, you're a pretty good singer and guitar player; why don't you teach music." Then someone else said, "And you're an athlete, and you've been studying yoga, so why don't you do yoga, meditation and athletics with the kids?"

It was settled. I became a teacher of music, meditation, yoga, and sports during recess. My goal for music was for each child to know that they had a song in them, and I would help them find this song, write the lyrics, and put a tune to the words. My goal for yoga and meditation was for each child to discover the quiet center of their being and know how to return to it when necessary. And my goal for sports was for everyone to fulfill their own physical potential while playing cooperatively with each other.

It was all so different from my own schooling where I struggled with my schoolwork and cobbled together an awkward identity from what my teachers and parents told me. It was absolutely amazing to be part of a team of teachers, working together for the sake of the children. A child would bring a poem from their writing class to the music room and we would put it to music. Kids who loved music, but who had a hard time with math, would learn mathematical intervals between the notes in a chord. Kids with special interests apprenticed with adults in town to learn painting, pottery, skiing, photography, rock climbing and biology. It was the best year of my life, and the first time I felt liked for who I was, and who I aspired to become, and not for who I was raised and educated to be.

One of our most audacious experiments was to begin the school with no rules, only a class schedule. We let the children know from day one that this was *their* school, and it was up to *them* to create the rules. We figured that they would have a unique sense of ownership and personal responsibility if they made the rules. We hoped they would realize that we respected them and had confidence in their ability to govern themselves. Needless to say, the school was in a state of pandemonium for the first two weeks of its existence! Kids were running around, shouting and reveling in their new-found freedom. It was everything their previous school experience was not, and they loved it . . . for a while. Just as we were beginning to question the sanity of having no rules, something amazing happened. One morning, at our all-school meeting, one child after another began to complain about the noise and commotion that accompanied almost every minute of the day. Then, one by one, they agreed that what the school needed was rules. And they made them—the same rules we would have imposed—but they were *their* rules, and they stuck to them.

During those tumultuous first weeks of school, my music and yoga room was an oasis of calm. Each morning, about eight kids would come in to start the day. Some of the boys were hyperactive, while most of the girls were more naturally introspective. We started class with a fifteen-minute series of yoga poses. Then we all sat down in a circle. To quiet their minds, I led them in simple breathing exercises. Then, with eyelids half-opened, we focused on a symbol or simple object that I would place in the middle of the circle. We would sit for about 10 minutes, breathing and focusing on the object in front of us, then I would remind them that they could always return to this calm, centered state of mind when they were sick, injured, or worried. I reminded them to treat each other with kindness throughout the day, and to treat each other like they would like to be treated by others. Then we would talk for a few minutes about what came up for them during our yoga and meditation. I asked them to accept and observe all these passing mental events and let them go while focusing on their breathing.

With their minds calm and quiet, the kids would go into their other activities with a new spirit. Even the hyperactive kids were amazingly calm and prepared to go quietly to their next class. Teaching yoga and meditation to these nine to twelve year-olds was an extraordinary experience for me. It confirmed my belief that even children could become familiar with the deep and abiding center within them, and that once found, they would be less likely to flit desperately from one sensory object to the next in search of happiness and fulfillment. We didn't need to talk about religion or spirituality, because once they had nourished the seed of contemplative consciousness in them, they naturally developed an interest in the spiritual dimensions of religion.

After a short time, our team of teachers gathered to talk about the learning styles of the children. Then, based on what we had seen, we began to customize a curriculum that would allow each child to master the essential knowledge and skills mandated by the State of Colorado. We developed practical and fun projects that required students to learn new skills in math, science, reading and writing. Working in this way, we didn't have to discipline kids who were bored or acting-out because they weren't able to engage with impersonal methods of teaching. It was *their* method, *their* way of learning. This approach was more fun and engaging for the teachers as well, saving them from the tedium of unchanging lesson plans.

This environment helped me recognize that my own personal learning style was primarily metaphysical. Since childhood, I had always been interested in the 'why' of things. I wanted to know why the universe existed, why I existed, and why people suffered. I wanted to know what happens when we die, and if my own identity would be lost. When it came to mathematics, I cared less about memorizing theorems than knowing why they were invented and what grander purpose they served. Through teaching in this environment, I realized that the public school curriculum hadn't worked for me because my personal learning style was not recognized and accommodated. I was asking questions that they were not interested in answering. Thus, it was difficult for me to achieve anything better than Bs and Cs, while many friends easily earned As and Bs.

The work and experiments we made in that critical first year were intended to set a moral tone and intention that would provide the school with a solid foundation. And today, after more than forty years, I am happy to report that the Aspen Community School is still alive as a public charter school in Colorado.

Doctoral Degree in Buddhist Studies

While I was in India, the Dalai Lama had advised me to continue my studies in America with Geshe Lhundup Sopa, who had recently joined the faculty of the University of Wisconsin-Madison. Thus, I traveled to Wisconsin to meet him, and being greatly impressed, began to seriously consider studying for a Ph.D. in Buddhist Studies under him.

On the surface, this seemed like an absurd idea. My grades in high school and college were never more than average, and I was a poor standardized test taker. Moreover, my foreign language skills were ordinary, at best, and studying Buddhism at this level would require me to learn both Tibetan and Sanskrit! So it seemed rather audacious to think that I could even get into graduate school, much less succeed there. Nevertheless, I was buoyed by memories of past successes in subjects with which I found a real connection and passion, as well as by my experiences with The Aspen Community School. I was confident that my sincere motivation to learn Buddhism would empower me to learn even those things for which I had shown no previous aptitude.

I moved to Madison in the summer of 1972 and into a tiny basement bedroom in my teacher's house. In order to qualify for in-state tuition, I got a Wisconsin driver's license and began working as a furniture mover. With Geshe Sopa, I began studying Tibetan by reading a simple text on Buddhist philosophy along with the classical Tibetan language textbook he was then writing. Every other day, we sat down as teacher and student to review my studies. Every evening, we ate dinner together and talked about Buddhist philosophy and practice. Each morning and evening, I would practice the Buddhist meditation that I had begun in India.

When the time came to apply to graduate school, I made an appointment with the dean to plead my case. I told him that it was unlikely that I would qualify for admission by the ordinary standards, but that I had been studying hard for the past year and knew that I could be successful in the program. I begged him for a chance to prove myself. After some consideration, he agreed to let me in on probation, telling me that I had to get straight A's or I would be out. I promised him that I would get the grades and I was admitted to the program.

I worked hard and succeeded. But, in my second year of

graduate school, I failed to get an A in one course. For my minor, I had chosen philosophy, another subject for which I had shown no previous aptitude, and in a difficult course on the philosophy of Immanuel Kant, I received a B+. Fortunately, the dean didn't seem to notice, or by that time, didn't care!

While graduate school was a huge challenge for me, I was totally engrossed in and committed to my studies. The biggest difficulty was learning Sanskrit, the ancient language of India, and the scriptural language of Mahayana Buddhism. I spent many hours each week, late into the night, learning the grammar, syntax, and vocabulary of the most highly inflected language in the world. As I studied the structure of Sanskrit, I realized that I was also learning how to think logically. All the parts of speech that had eluded me in high school English now began to make sense. I realized that I wasn't just learning an ancient language through which I would learn Buddhism, I was actually learning how to think!

Perhaps most gratifying of all was my growing confidence in the fact that I didn't suffer from an inherent, incurable intellectual disability, as I had previously thought. I was like one of those kids I had taught in the Aspen Community School, gaining confidence in my innate abilities and set free for the first time. I felt I could do almost anything in which I believed passionately, with my whole heart and head.

In my second year of graduate school, I was awarded a teaching assistantship to help Geshe Sopa prepare materials for his classes. This was especially rewarding as it enabled me to work closely with him, translating Tibetan Buddhist technical terms into English. We were then making the first generation of Tibetan Buddhist translations into English for a culture that knew almost nothing about the subject. It was an exhilarating process of discovery, translating and transmitting this ancient culture and religious tradition for the modern world.

During these years, I also discovered that Buddhism makes room for a variety of learning styles. It is the job of a good Buddhist teacher is to recognize the style of each student and to adapt his or her own teaching accordingly. Buddhism stresses that every individual has the capacity to become enlightened, and that there are a variety of different paths. While some of these styles are developmental, others seem to be imbedded in the fundamental personality of the student. For example, Buddhism identifies three types of spiritual seeker: the *bodhisattva,* who is primarily motivated by compassion; the *shravaka,* who is primarily a listener; and the *pratyekabuddha,* who is someone who studies alone without a teacher and a community of students.

Some Tibetan Buddhist traditions even prescribe specific practices that align with the relative influence of each of the five elements on the psycho-physical makeup of each student. Thus, the elements of earth, fire, air, water and ether each carry a set of personality characteristics and learning predispositions that should be factored into the teaching and learning process.

Another set of types is defined in the *Lam Rim,* or 'stages of the path' teachings of various Tibetan Buddhist traditions. In these teachings, students are classified developmentally, according to their purpose and intention for study and practice. The first stage is for students who are only concerned with obtaining a higher rebirth in the next life. The second stage is for students who are concerned with emancipation from the rounds of birth and rebirth, and desire nothing less than *nirvana,* freedom from the causes of suffering and eternal bliss. The third stage is for students who wish nothing less than the emancipation and enlightenment of all beings, and who are thus dedicated to enlightenment for themselves in order to achieve that altruistic aim. Thus, it is clear that this classification focuses on intention—not ability. It presupposes that all individuals have the potential to become perfectly enlightened and liberated Buddhas, if it is their intention to do so. Thus, it is also an intention that changes the dynamic of learning and is the grounding for actualizing our most profound potential.

After three and half years of course work, I successfully passed my examinations and received approval for my thesis topic. As a Fulbright Fellow, I headed to India to study in the Tibetan refugee monasteries with great Tibetan teachers who could not speak a word of English. My job was to translate and analyze the compassion section of a great commentary on the *Perfection of Wisdom Sutra,* the foundational text of Mahayana Buddhism.

While living in these monasteries, I observed that the monks were allowed to gravitate naturally to the type of study and practice that best suited their temperaments. There were many practices that everyone had to do together, but there were also specialized areas, such as ritual, religious art, meditation, building, cooking, or administration, which monks could take-up based on their own personalities and predispositions. Each person was respected for the work they did, especially if they did it diligently and well.

As I traveled throughout India, I also began to observe the marvelous variety of religious expressions and paths of spiritual practice. It was as if this great variety of deities, worship and spiritual practice had evolved to accommodate the spiritual styles of every type of person. You see it in the depictions of deities who seem to represent all the different aspects of the divine. You see it in the faces of religious people who attend the temples, bathe in the sacred rivers, attend lectures, study the ancient scriptures, perform the rituals, songs, dances and chants. You see it in the vocations of healers, wandering ascetics, philosophers and meditators. Over the millennia, India has become a vibrant spiritual culture that accepts the full variety of religious ideas, styles and practices.

During my stay in Varanasi, the holy city of India, I studied and conferred with some of India's most highly regarded philosophers and spiritual teachers, including exponents of Vedanta, who teach that there are four primary types of spiritual teaching and practice. The first, Karma Yoga, is designed for people who aspire to be engaged actively in society by helping to improve the lives of others. The second, Bhakti Yoga, recognizes that there are people who are motivated by deep faith and devotion toward spiritual deities, teachers and goals. The third, Jnana Yoga, is the path of those who need to use their intellectual faculties to develop a spiritual practice that conforms to reason. The fourth, Raja Yoga, pertains to those who are predisposed to the deepest practices of contemplation and meditation. This system recognizes that each individual contains all four predispositions in varying degrees, and that a fully mature person might actualize them all in equal measure.

I could not help but contrast the rich and energetic spiritual life of India with what seemed to me to be the comparatively narrow scope of American religion at the time. One simply did not see the same vibrancy and spiritual expression, nor the same openness to different spiritual paths and practices. It seemed to me that the crisis of faith experienced by many Americans could be blamed on the lack of openness to the full spectrum of spiritual experience, and the failure to recognize the wonderful variety of spiritual approaches available to suit different spiritual predispositions.

CREATING THE SPIRITUAL PATHS MANDALA

Since then, the exploration of different spiritual learning styles has become a passion for me. After I finished my Ph.D., I continued to research various belief systems and learning modalities in my careers as a documentary filmmaker through the 1970s, as a program director at the Smithsonian Institution in the 1980s, and even as a businessman running an internet company in the 1990s.

In 1997, I was honored with an invitation from Father Thomas Keating to be the Buddhist participant in the highly-respected Snowmass Interreligious Conference, an annual retreat at which contemplative leaders from different religious traditions sit together in meditation and deep dialogue about their respective spiritual practices and experiences. Although I had been interested in interfaith work for some time, I really had no idea that there existed such extraordinary commonalities between the great contemplative traditions. It also became clear—much to my surprise—that most of the world's religions have deep and profound traditions of meditation. At Snowmass, we practiced our own respective meditations together in silence.

It was during these extraordinary meditation sessions that I first began to feel a kind of 'InterSpiritual Consciousness' emerging among us in the silence. By experiencing and dialoguing about one another's spiritual practices, I found that each of us was helped to discover new depths in our own individual practices. Thus, I began to see that the religions of the world were not isolated institutions at all, but interdependent phenomena within a vast spiritual eco-system. It was this revelation that led me to envision the Spiritual Paths Foundation, in which I could to bring together my personal interests in meditation, interfaith dialogue, and spiritual learning styles for the first time.

Not long after, I sold my business and began devoting all my energy to the creation of the Spiritual Paths Foundation. This gave me the time to reexamine a process of spiritual education and practice I had begun developing ten years earlier while working at the Smithsonian. I proposed that all of us, everywhere, have predominate spiritual learning styles and fundamental spiritual questions, and that our personal spiritual paths are conditioned by these styles and questions. Thus, I hoped that the Spiritual Paths Foundation might develop programs and materials to help each person discern and piece together their own unique path.

In 2000, I began to seek the advice and wisdom of spiritual elders like Father Thomas Keating, Geshe Sopa, Rabbi Zalman Schachter-Shalomi, and numerous other colleagues and friends. I also set about building a unique internet-based resource to facilitate the seeker's inquiry, and created the first offerings of the Spiritual Paths Institute, a series of InterSpiritual seminars for the public. These were to be modeled on the dialogue of the Snowmass Conference.

To each seminar, I invited teachers from the world's great spiritual traditions to spend several days together with a group of students. In the course of these days, we meditated together, shared meals, formed friendships, and began a private dialogue that culminated in a public seminar. At the seminar, each teacher gave their own perspective on the particular spiritual theme (i.e., spiritual style or question) and later participated in a focused InterSpiritual dialogue before an audience. After the audience had heard all the speakers, they were given the opportunity to ask questions of the speaker who had touched them most in a smaller group setting. In this way, we could explore themes and questions from many different spiritual perspectives and in a very personal way.

We held our first Spiritual Paths seminar on "The Way of Contemplation and Mediation" in Aspen, Colorado in July of 2002. Since then, we have presented over a hundred courses and classes, taught by more than fifty teachers. These collaborations, along with my own private teaching, have given me the opportunity to test my original hypothesis with great teachers from a variety of traditions, and with students of all backgrounds.

I have learned that every religion contains a wonderful diversity of educational methods and spiritual practices, formulated for particular types of individuals and their different learning styles. Therefore, it only makes sense to engage and explore our own personal learning styles and spiritual questions in a purposeful way, as a prerequisite and primary means of discovering which teachings and practices are most compatible with those styles and questions, and not the other way around.

I conceived of a *mandala*—a picture of spiritual wholeness—in which I could bring together twelve archetypal learning styles, twelve spiritual questions, and twelve spiritual and secular wisdom traditions, each offering distinctive answers to those questions, along with teachings and practices suitable to different learning styles. These sets of twelve styles, questions, and traditions were then placed upon three concentric rings in a circle, with the center representing the essence of one's own personal spiritual path. I called this the Spiritual Paths (or InterSpiritual) Mandala. The actual form and shapes in the Mandala diagram came to me during an imaginal journey to a remote valley in Central Asia. (See Appendix X for a description of this imaginal journey.)

Why twelve? Why not eleven or thirteen sets of styles, questions and traditions in the Spiritual Paths Mandala? In truth, there could be more or less, depending on one's method for defining and categorizing them. Twelve is simply a number that worked for me in organizing this process. I look at these as twelve families of spiritual styles, questions and traditions, or twelve broadly defined categories into which other subcategories can be inserted. The primary purpose here is educational, to help students discover their own styles for spiritual learning, and harness them to find the answers, teachers, traditions and practices that suit their natural spiritual predispositions.

The real issue is the difficulty many of us have in developing a coherent and sustainable spiritual path today. My thesis is that the cause for this difficulty is a disconnect between our own archetypal learning styles and the ways spiritual teachings and practices have been presented to us. This disconnect is similar to the problem I encountered with the one-size-fits-all approach to educating children, who actually represent a variety of different learning styles. Thus, some children failed to thrive, not because they were stupid, but because the teacher or system insisted on presenting material in a way that did not connect with their natural learning style.

When it comes to spirituality, there are a variety of methods for organizing and presenting information. These methods of presentation and teaching reflect the archetypal styles of the organizers and teachers of the information. They also represent institutional approaches to spiritual education and practice. Therefore, depending on the writer or the institution, the same doctrinal material is presented from a variety of perspectives, including the arts, the body, meditation, mysticism, nature, reason, and prayer.

There is a remarkable similarity between the tone and content of specific genres of spiritual literature from one tradition to another. This similarity is not necessarily an indication that all religions are indeed 'one,' as some would claim, but rather a reflection of the primary spiritual styles of the individuals who wrote them. This means that writers whose style is 'mystical,' no matter what their religion may be called, tend to view the world through very similar lenses, and to interpret religious and spiritual experiences in much the same way. Therefore, if one were to ignore the title of the book, or the name of the particular deity mentioned in it, it would be difficult to distinguish the actual religion of one mystical writer from another. You might even think they all belong to the same religion. But actually, it is the archetypal style that they have in common—they all follow the Way of the Mystic. We could observe the same phenomenon with religious thinkers who process spiritual phenomena, for example, through the Way of Reason, or the Way of Nature, or the Way of the Arts.

This insight shows us that it is crucially important to discover and harness our own personal spiritual styles in order to find the teachings and practices that will best satisfy our personal spiritual needs. For example, the teachings and practices that represent the Way of Reason in any tradition are never going to satisfy someone whose primary path is that of the Mystic. But once one's primary learning style is honored, there is a vast and fascinating diversity of teachers and resources available across the spectrum of our collective spiritual traditions to help one further refine a personal spiritual path.

Although each of us has a learning style that best suit our needs, all twelve archetypal styles dwell within us as possibilities, and all these influence our spiritual paths in one way or another. There is no qualitative hierarchy of learning styles, and no people who embody just one learning style. For example, living in a body, we cannot wholly ignore the Way of the Body, even if our primary style might be imaginal or intellectual. Often one style that is dominant at one point in our lives will be less important at another.

These styles might be thought of as 'funnels' through which information is channeled for processing and analysis, like sieves that catch certain types of information for the mind; or perhaps, colored lenses that determine the hue of the world before our eyes. While each style focuses our attention and enables us to begin our quest via devotion, mysticism, intellection, etc., an exclusive emphasis on that Way also limits our ability to totally perceive and experience the wholeness of our spiritual potential. Therefore, it is important to recognize that our 'dominant style' may only be a beginning-point. From it, we might expand and make use of all the other styles to achieve the fullest and most complete experience of the spiritual path.*

There may be times in our lives when we are more devotional or more intellectual. Occasionally, we might have a mystical experience. At other times, our styles lead us to be more physical or interpersonal. As we go through life's changes and our dominant mode of learning or inclination changes, we need different and specific kinds of resources to help. Wouldn't it be wonderful if such resources were available as soon as the inspiration and need arises? If we are forced to wait, precious opportunities for spiritual growth might be lost or squandered. Now, with the ubiquity of the Internet, translations of previously hidden books, and availability of teachers from all traditions, our opportunities for spiritual growth have multiplied. Thus, our current challenge is to employ a methodology for accessing and applying the wealth of knowledge to our personal lives. Hopefully, the Spiritual Paths Mandala will help satisfy this need.

In the following pages, we will explore each of the twelve spiritual styles and questions, and I will attempt to illustrate them with episodes from my own life and examples of my own process on the Buddhist path and engagement with other spiritual teachers and traditions. It is my hope that these examples will give you some sense of how you might engage in this process yourself. As you read the sections of the book, I would suggest that you begin to journal on each of these styles and questions, exploring how each is expressed in your own life. In so doing, you may discover your own personal spiritual path in one tradition, or from among a variety of traditions. And if you would like still more support in discerning your path, you might also consider taking advantage of different Spiritual Paths seminars, retreats, online courses or the InterSpiritual Mentor Training program. This way, you will not

---

* Each of these archetypal styles also implies a genre of spiritual practice that will propel us along our spiritual path. So as we discern and give voice to each style, we also are led to the practices that best fit that style. Therefore, there is a direct relationship between discerning our styles and harnessing those styles in the form of compatible practices.

only create your own path but help others experience the joy and fulfillment of creating theirs.

OVERVIEW OF THE
SPIRITUAL PATHS MANDALA

IN THE MID 1990s, the Tibetan Buddhist abbot, Geshe Lobsang Tenzin, came to visit me at my home in Woody Creek, Colorado. A master of both the exoteric and esoteric *(sutra* and *tantra)* traditions of Buddhism whom I had first met in India, Geshe-la had been helping to mold my intellectual understanding and spiritual practice since the mid-1970s.

Buddhism first came to Tibet during the 7th-century C.E., more than a thousand years after the death of the Buddha. It came in various forms and traditions from both China and India, and a succession of Tibetan rulers sponsored a massive effort to translate hundreds of Buddhist scriptures into the Tibetan language.

Because of the many differences and apparent contradictions within these Buddhist scriptures, an effort was made to determine how they all could be the correct and authentic teachings of the Buddha. One major explanation said that different scriptures were delivered to students of varying intentions and mental capacities. The least developed students, it said, were only interested in religion to achieve a good reincarnation. Students of middling capacity wanted to be free from the cycle of birth and rebirth altogether. The students of highest capacity were those striving to achieve Enlightenment in order to help others to be free from suffering.

Another explanation for the apparent contradictions came in the form of the metaphor of the wise doctor who administers different medicine depending on the individual needs of the patient. What is medicine for one patient might be poison for another. Therefore, the scriptures were organized around "stages of the path" that would gradually lead students to higher and higher spiritual teachings and practices according to their intention and capacity. Buddhist teachers thus became skilled at identifying the predispositions of their students so they could provide just the right teachings at the right time. Since there is an extensive oral tradition to accompany the written scriptures, skillful teachers also customized their teachings for students of various learning predispositions so that they could understand difficult Buddhist concepts and practices.**

Through Tibetan Buddhist teachers like Geshe Lobsang Tenzin, I have learned to be sensitive to the 'learning styles' of different students, and aware of how their styles can be vehicles for progress along the spiritual path.

During Geshe-la's visit, we were invited to St. Benedict's Monastery in Snowmass, Colorado, to give a brief talk and engage in an interfaith dialogue. I was to be Geshe-la's translator—a job I found difficult, as I hadn't spoken Tibetan for some time. Nevertheless, the dialogue went well and we were invited to attend Sunday Mass shortly thereafter.

It was the Sunday before Easter, and the small chapel was packed with hundreds of people. When the time came for Holy Communion, everyone gathered near the front of the chapel in a semi-circle around the modest, rustic altar.

Just before Communion began, Father Theophane, one of the most revered monks in the monastery, approached Geshe-la and me. He was wore a floor-length white robe, a distinguished gray beard, and walked with a stooped posture that made him look like an ancient medieval mendicant. In spite of his appearance, his quick wit and casual manner always made everyone feel at ease.

Father Theophane leaned forward and whispered in my ear, "Some of the more 'conservative' members of the congregation may not be comfortable if Geshe-la joins in Communion. Do you think he would mind not participating?"

I conveyed this to Geshe-la and he replied that he was happy to stand back and observe. They looked each other in the eye for

---

* On this subject, the Dalai Lama had this to say: [. . .] the Buddha knew the different mental dispositions of his followers. The main purpose of teaching religion is to help people, not to become famous, so he taught what was suitable according to the disposition of his listeners. So even Buddha Shakyamuni very much respected the views and rights of individuals. A teaching may be profound but if it does not suit a particular person, what is the use of explaining it? In this sense, the dharma is like medicine. The main value of medicine is that it cures illness [. . .] if it is not appropriate for the patient, then it is of no use. (His Holiness the Dalai Lama , *The Four Noble Truths* (1997), 5-6.)

a moment and their smiles told me that they shared a deeper understanding of the nature of the ritual and a similar conviction that there was no point in offending the fundamentalists in the congregation. Still, I thought it would have been a remarkable sight to see a Tibetan Buddhist monk in red robes taking Holy Communion from a Christian monk!

As I watched and participated in the Eucharist, I was moved by feelings of the sacred, reminiscent of the awe and mystery I had experienced in the Buddhist monastery presided over by Geshe-la. In his monastery, he would have been seated on a high throne-like seat where everyone could see him performing intricate mudras (symbolic hand gestures), handling various ritual objects and chanting in a deep, loud voice. When Geshe-la performed these rituals, he was actually embodying the body, speech and mind of the Buddha, and the ritual was the process for manifesting this embodiment. Similarly, every other Tibetan monk in the temple visualized themselves as becoming Buddhas. These Tibetan Buddhist tantric rituals are radical acts of personal transformation designed to quicken the spiritual evolution of each participant.

Here in the chapel of St. Benedict's, we stood among hundreds of people watching Father Thomas Keating embodying the spirit of Christ as he recited from scripture and held high the wafer of bread and the goblet of wine: "This is my body, which is for you: do this in remembrance of me . . . This cup is the new covenant in my blood, drink in remembrance of me."

For the first time in my life, I recognized the esoteric purpose of the Christian Eucharist. It was not just to "remember" Jesus, but for some, to actually become 'one with Christ.' In this sense, the Eucharist might be seen as a Christian tantric rite! It is not merely a ritual to be done by rote, but an active process of embodying the mind, body, and spirit of Christ!

The monks of St. Benedict's Monastery are famous both for their dedication to contemplative practice and for their ecumenism. Father Thomas Keating, a former abbot now residing at St. Benedict's, is the one of the founders of the Centering Prayer Movement that has revived the contemplative traditions of *The Cloud of Unknowing*, St. John of the Cross and other Christian contemplatives. The meditative techniques of Centering Prayer have much in common with Buddhist mindfulness meditation. Thus, the atmosphere at St. Benedict's is extremely peaceful, open and accepting. The monks are curious about the diverse faiths of their visitors and generally willing to share their own faith in a gentle, non-didactic fashion.

Like a number of those present, I was not Catholic, but did participate in the Eucharist. As I looked around at the congregation surrounding the altar, the faces and body language of each person told me a lot about their spiritual style. Perhaps I was projecting, but I was nevertheless able to observe how each of the twelve spiritual predispositions seemed to be operating in the individuals in the chapel.

Some of the people were clearly moved by the *artistic* or *aesthetic* ambience of the environs. They seemed to enjoy, to be comforted and inspired by the atmosphere of the chapel, with its candles, the sounds of the chants, the holy objects, the light filtering in through stained glass windows, the austere architecture with its gray walls, arched ceiling, wooden benches and stone floor. From the peaceful looks on their faces and their relaxed postures, I could tell that this awakened the spiritual Way of the Arts within them, and helped them to immerse in the mystery of the Eucharist.

Others, whose spiritual style was *kinesthetic* or *somatic* seemed to feel this profound mystery in their bodies by participating in the movements of the service. The kneeling, making the sign of the cross, standing in communion with others, reverently approaching the altar, holding the cup and wafer, eating and drinking all resonated with that part of their being.

In still others, I observed a predisposition toward *contemplation* and *meditation*. They appeared to be very much within themselves. Though present and attentive, it was clear that they were not fixed on the exterior form of the Eucharist, but rather on something deep within themselves. By the introspective look on their faces and the relaxed manner of their bodies, I could tell that this mode of processing the Eucharist was natural to them.

Then there were others whose spiritual style was *devotional* and I could clearly see this in the look on their faces and in the way their hands were held reverently near their hearts. For them, the Eucharist was an opportunity to express their faith, both privately and publicly. It seemed to help them feel the Grace of the Holy Spirit and give them strength, knowing that this honest, sincere expression of faith would manifest the presence of the Father, Son and Holy Spirit in their lives. They seemed to be experiencing that quiet, ecstatic joy that results from moments of pure devotion.

Then there were those devotionally minded folks who clearly saw the *ritual* as a central feature of their faith. While participating in the Eucharist seemed deeply satisfying to everyone in the congregation, it was especially important for those for whom predictability and repetition is crucial to their spiritual life. The mere fact that one can count on the predictable performance of this spiritual re-affirmation gives comfort and meaning to life. Ritual brings us together with those we love and respect, and with whom we share common values. Rituals create a safe, shared space where we can re-commit ourselves to our highest aspirations.

There were also a few who were standing back in an observing, *intellectual* mode. They didn't have the look of skepticism or critical doubt, but did seem to be analyzing the structure of the ritual, the objects that were used and the words and gestures of the priest. I could see signs of satisfaction on their faces, as though they had gained an understanding of a conceptual framework in which the Eucharist took on a useful meaning and purpose for them.

Others in the congregation appeared to approach the Eucharist through a *mystical* mode of consciousness. Communion for them evoked a sense of spiritual identity or oneness with the Holy Spirit. The taking of bread and wine were a powerful psychological and physical means to embody the qualities of Christ—to become 'Christ-like.' They were attracted by the magic, mystery and alchemy of the Eucharist. Like the metaphorical alchemical transformation of lead into gold, they were experiencing the transmutation of the dark and heavy material consciousness of normal daily life into the brilliant golden light of Christ-consciousness.

Likewise, others were responding to the Eucharist based on the *images* it stimulated in their minds and the psychological impact of these images, evoking beauty, love, compassion, kindness, forgiveness and sacrifice. While they might not have been fully conscious of these interior images, they were emotionally responding to the resonance of both their internal imagination and the external imagery of the chapel.

The symbolic images in the church—the cross, the tree, the dove, the virgin mother, the lamb, the chalice, the snake—help to reinforce and give power to the archetype of the Christ. The ritual of the Eucharist brings the Christ archetype to the surface of the mind. In so doing, it can align the other archetypes, transforming them to the noble aspirations of a Christ. The internal and external images of the Eucharist help one to become Christ-like, to become one with the Holy Spirit.

Then there were people whose spiritual style was clearly based on their *relationship* with friends, spouses and companions gathered in the chapel. Their relationship with Christ was strengthened through their relationship with other believers. Taking communion in community was a way of strengthening this relationship, for it is through these relationships that they evolve toward individual and collective spiritual fulfillment.

Clearly, each of the twelve spiritual archetypes provided people in the chapel with personal entry-points into the Eucharist and the creation of their own spiritual path. These styles are like lenses or filters through which they mentally processed the sensory data of the ritual and then channel it toward the actualization of their spiritual aspirations. While many people processed the ritual according to one or two archetypal styles, others might have been absorbed through all twelve simultaneously. Therefore, all potentialities within their consciousness could be engaged in holistic spiritual experience. This coming together and alignment of all our archetypal spiritual styles brings-on the full integration and actualization of our human spiritual potential. This holistic integration of all archetypal spiritual styles, it seems to me, is the hallmark of a fully actualized spiritual being.

THE SPIRITUAL PATHS MANDALA

Here is a brief overview of the Mandala and its three sets of twelve spiritual styles, spiritual questions, and spiritual traditions. The outer circle illustrates twelve spiritual archetypes or styles, each of which represents a number of similar predispositions or lenses collected under one name or archetype. The middle circle illustrates twelve spiritual questions, or rather a 'family' of related questions summed-up by the headings in the circle. The inner circle illustrates twelve spiritual, philosophical and scientific traditions from which we draw teachings and practices for our particular style, and answers to our particular questions. The white circle in the center indicates your own personal inner path, the sum total of knowledge and practices you have collected and followed.

The following chart lists each of these three sets of twelve families of archetypal styles, questions and traditions.*

SPIRITUAL STYLES, QUESTIONS, AND TRADITIONS

	ARCHETYPAL STYLES	QUESTIONS	TRADITIONS
1	Arts (The Artist)	Consciousness	Buddhism
2	Body (The Kinesthete)	Death	Christianity
3	Devotion (The Devotee)	Existence	Hinduism
4	Imagination (The Dreamer)	Freedom	Islam
5	Love (The Lover)	God	Judaism
6	Meditation (The Meditator)	Good & Evil	African
7	Mystic (The Mystic)	Happiness	Asian
8	Nature (The Naturalist)	Reality	American
9	Prayer (The Prayer)	Soul	European
10	Reason (The Thinker)	Spirit-Beings	Middle Eastern
11	Relationship (The Mensch)	Suffering	Oceanic
12	Wisdom (The Sage)	Transformation & Ultimate Potential	Science, Philosophy, Mythology

---

* In the chart above, the style and question columns are listed in alphabetical order. The tradition column begins with the five major religions followed by seven geographical areas of origin for other religions and secular traditions. In the Mandala discernment process, each student will line up their own personal styles and questions according to the tradition(s) in which they seek answers.

THE ARCHETYPAL STYLES

For brevity's sake, each of the twelve archetypal styles are described by a single word in the Mandala, but should be understood as "The Way of the Arts," "The Way of the Body," and so on. Furthermore, each of the twelve represents a broader family of spiritual archetypes. For example, the Path of Devotion also represents faith and belief. The purpose of this list of twelve is not to be comprehensive, but inclusive. They are meant to prompt you to ask yourself such questions as: How do I learn? What is my spiritual archetype? What is my spiritual style? During the course of your life, your primary and contributing archetypes will change. Each is like a tributary flowing into the river of life, or branches of a trail that all join into a single life-path.

THE QUESTIONS

The simple, one-word descriptions for each of the twelve spiritual questions likewise represent a family of related questions. These are the 'big questions' we begin asking as children. They are also the perennial, universal questions asked by scientists, philosophers and theologians. For example, the question of consciousness covers a host of questions, like: What is mind? How do I know? Is consciousness produced by the brain? What is the ultimate potential of consciousness? The questions listed here are only meant to inspire you to ask your own questions and to embrace the mysteries that await the discoveries that will define your own spiritual path.

THE TRADITIONS

This process for discerning your own archetypal style, honoring your own questions, and finding your own answers can be pursued within a single spiritual tradition or among a variety of traditions. Among those listed are the five major religious traditions, six named for their geographical place of origin, and one which includes the secular traditions of philosophy, science, psychology and mythology. Whether your path is formed within one tradition or many, this Mandala is designed to help you engage in a life-long adventure of exploration and discovery of your own personal path.

A SUMMARY OF THE TWELVE STYLES

1. "The Artist" — The Way of the Arts

   The Artist finds spiritual inspiration, beauty, as well as personal expression through painting, drawing, sculpture, music, dance or poetry.

2. "The Kinesthete" — The Way of the Body

   The Kinesthete uses physical movement as a primary mode of learning and experiences subtle emotional and spiritual states of consciousness in various parts of their body.

3. "The Contemplative" or "Meditator" — The Way of Contemplation and Meditation

   The Contemplative or Meditator is drawn to quiet and solitary introspection and seeks to discover the truth within or through communion with the numinous.

4. "The Devotee" — The Way of Devotion

   The Devotee is naturally loyal and lovingly committed to a job, a relationship, a set of principles, a way of life, a daily routine, a religious teacher, a spiritual tradition or a life-goal.

5. "The Dreamer" — The Way of Imagination

   The Dreamer naturally dwells in the imaginary awareness of possibility, intrigued by images arising from the limitless depths of consciousness.

6. "The Lover" — The Way of Love and Compassion

   The Lover naturally experiences the universality of love and seeks to bring happiness and relief to the suffering of others.

7. "The Mystic" — The Way of the Mystic

   The Mystic naturally feels, intuits, communes with or otherwise experiences the mysteries of the numinous that lie beyond the boundaries of ordinary human perception.

8. "The Naturalist" — The Way of Nature

The Naturalist is most at ease when surrounded by nature, whether in the forest, the desert, the plains, the mountains, streams, lakes or the oceans of the natural environment, in harmony with all the shared elements of existence.

9. "The Prayer" — The Way of Prayer

The Prayer naturally seeks wisdom, guidance, help, strength, healing or forgiveness from a sacred being or divine source whose capabilities supersede those of ordinary human beings.

10. "The Thinker" — The Way of Reason

The Thinker needs to figure things out and to create a reasonable foundation for all aspects of spiritual practice.

11. "The Mensch" — The Way of Relationships

The Mensch learns most naturally and expresses spirituality through compassionate interaction with others, gaining deep satisfaction thereby.

12. "The Sage" — The Way of Wisdom

The Sage embodies the wisdom of a life fully-lived and the truths transmitted by profound wisdom-holders throughout the ages.

A SUMMARY OF THE TWELVE QUESTIONS

1. Consciousness

Is my mind confined to my brain and nervous system? Is my personal conscious connected to a larger, perhaps universal sphere of consciousness?

2. Death

What happens to my consciousness when my body dies? Is death the end of me?

3. Existence

Is there a beginning or end to existence? How and why do I exist? Did life evolve, or was it originally created by a pre-existing God or divine force?

4. Freedom

   Is it possible to be free from the struggles of normal life? What would total freedom look like?

5. God

   Is there a divine creator or creative energy behind all that exists?

6. Good & Evil

   What is 'the good'? Do I need wisdom to be good? Do I need to be good to be happy? Are there countervailing forces of good and evil in the world?

7. Happiness

   Is happiness the same as fun and enjoyment? What is true happiness and how can I achieve it?

8. Reality

   Does the world around me exist in the way I perceive it? How much of the external world is created by my own bias and projection?

9. Soul

   Is there an independent, eternal 'me' that experiences reality and can forge my own future? Do I have free will, or am I under the control of other forces?

10. Spirit-Beings

    Are there other intelligent, non-corporeal beings with whom I can communicate and possibly become?

11. Suffering

    What is suffering? What is the cause of suffering? Can we eliminate suffering? What is the cure for suffering?

12. Transformation & Ultimate Potential

    What is the highest potential for my existence? Do I have the potential to transform myself into my ideal being? Is it possible to become a Christ, Buddha, Moses, or an enlightened being? Is my natural state-of-being pure and enlightened? How should I engage in my own transformative process?

Twelve Spiritual Styles

What is the right path for you? In the terminology of the Mandala, the word 'path' does not refer to a religion, but to that course which best matches your own spiritual style, or combination of styles, containing your own personal answers to life's big questions. Your path might indeed be informed by the religion of your birth, or based upon a chosen faith tradition or a variety of religious, scientific and philosophical influences, but it is, nevertheless, *your path*.

As a first step on this journey, you might begin by keeping a journal in which you write your own thoughts about each of the styles, questions and traditions, how they relate to you, and how you might combine them into your own life's path. Such a journal can become an invaluable tool and resource as you go forward with this process. Indeed, this very book might be viewed as a model of this kind of journaling process, and may serve as a guide as you write your own spiritual autobiography.

Discerning Your Primary Spiritual Styles

In the back of this book, there is an abbreviated Spiritual Profiling Tool to help you discern your predominate spiritual styles.** But before you use this tool, it will be useful for you to read the more thorough descriptions of each of these archetypal styles in the chapters ahead. Having made a connection with one or more of the spiritual styles based on a thorough reading, you will find that your path will unfold much more naturally. As the old saying goes, "It takes two to Tango." When our internal subjective predispositions match an objective external set of spiritual teachings, then the dance really begins.

As I mentioned earlier, the longer you are on the path, other spiritual styles within you will also yearn to be engaged, allowing you to become a more fully actualized person. Like the Renaissance figures of old, who engaged in the arts, sciences, athletics, relationships and public service, we allow all twelve archetypal styles within us to find expression and satisfaction in the spiritual nature of our being. Gradually, over the course of a lifetime, our personal spiritual path is fully revealed.

---

* You can also engage with the complete profile tool and with a comprehensive course of study through on-line and in-person classes.

Since our archetypal spiritual styles are generally hidden from our conscious minds, they are often in control of our predisposition for, and attraction to certain spiritual ideas, practices, traditions, symbols, etc. The Mandala Process helps us to become aware of these styles and then consciously to use them in the development of our path. In other words, we harness our styles rather than being harnessed by them.

To help you engage in the development of your own path, I will provide a definition of each of the twelve styles and an example of how these have played-out in my own study and practice of Buddhism and engagement with other religions. I have found that writing about each of these has helped me to gain clarity and insight into my own path, so I hope you will do the same.

PART I
THE TWELVE SPIRITUAL STYLES

"THE ARTIST"
THE WAY OF THE ARTS

The Artist finds spiritual inspiration, beauty,
as well as personal expression through painting,
drawing, sculpture, music, dance or poetry.

Are you naturally comfortable with the creative or artistic expression?

Are there artists and works of art that give expression to your own sense of the spiritual?

Does participating in the arts inspire and bring-out the spiritual within you?

IF YOUR ANSWER to these questions is "Yes," then The Way of the Arts might be your primary road into spiritual learning and practice. For many artistic learners, spiritual experience is best conveyed through creative expression. Words and intellectual concepts often fail to capture, for example, an epiphany of the transcendent, the marvelous geometric designs of existence, the mysterious shapes and colors of creation, the beautiful galaxies of the universe. But in the poetry of Rumi, the music of Ravi Shankar, the kachina dance of the Hopi, or the paintings of Michelangelo, something of the grandeur and profundity of these experiences might be expressed. Our natural affinity for aesthetics inspires us to expand and deepen our own sense of the sacred.

Therefore, artists throughout the centuries have used symbols, sounds, colors, designs, metaphors, stories and movement as vehicles for awakening our sense of the sacred or numinous. While religions speak of God, Allah, Brahman, HaShem or Wakantanka, the arts allude to these supra-verbal realities through various modes of artistic expression. The arts can provide bridges to the sacred that normal conceptual modes cannot.

The Arts are also a means of creating a state of consciousness wherein the numinous can be perceived or intuited. Christian or Buddhist monastic chants, symphonic or choral music, Hindu devotional mantras, the whirling of dervishes, tribal drumming, dancing and sand painting, Japanese calligraphy, paintings, sculptures, tribal masks, religious architecture, and Taoist poetry are all art forms designed to engender a state of consciousness whereby transcendent communion with the numinous becomes possible.

As individuals, we are not only inspired by the arts, but personally explore and express our own spiritual musings and epiphanies through the art form most natural to us. We sing, dance, drum, chant, draw, paint or write poetry. Indeed, our very life can be an artistic expression of our deepest spiritual longings and realizations. Our way of being with others in our chosen professions and daily lives exudes an artistic beauty beyond sanctimonious attendance at weekly religious services. Thus, we might also call this The Way of Aesthetics, as this connotes a kind of *gestalt* wherein the art form itself and our state of consciousness resonate harmoniously to evoke a sense of awe, mystery and the sacred.

Engagement in an aesthetic experience also stimulates our innate capacity to focus without distraction on a single object of concentration. Through the arts, we are able to meander effortlessly into an abstract field of colors, shapes, sounds, words and movements and leave behind all other distractions. Even our anxieties and physical pains tend to disappear while we are absorbed in some aesthetic endeavor or experience. When we are in this tranquil, one-pointed state of consciousness, our physiology responds by relaxing, sometimes to the point of endorphin-induced ecstasy.

For many of us, aesthetic immersion can induce intuitions and epiphanies that may not arise through any other contemplative method or process. While spiritually-oriented artists might experience a divine mystery coming into form or melody though their art, an observer or listener might be inspired to experience a transcendent vision, feeling or parallel epiphany. Both the artist and the observer might experience peace, harmony, clarity, elation or bliss. Therefore, the Way of the Arts provides perhaps the most universal entry-point into the infinite potential of our being.

'Ah ha!' is often the verbal result of such experiences. It comes when something 'sinks-in' and one 'gets it.' The Way of the Arts can infuse the spheres of intellect, devotion, meditation and body with energetic inspiration. The artistic path can provide both an early glimpse, and possibly, a concluding epiphany to our quest for spiritual understanding, integration and transformation.

An inspired piece of spiritual art often emerges from those who have both cultivated an artistic skill and had a spiritual experience, say, of 'oneness,' interdependence, or the immanent presence of the sacred. Such a work of art can resonate deeply with others, expressing that which they might otherwise be unable to express. It can inspire us, strengthen us, and give us assurance that we are not alone in our inward quest for authentic experiences of something profoundly greater than ourselves.

Those of us who are not particularly skilled in the arts can still benefit from our own artistic expressions, even if they don't find an appreciative audience in the public. We can express ourselves in our journals, through poetry or songs, paintings or dance. But our most profound personal art form is expressed in the way we live our own lives. For if we intentionally live our lives as expressions of our deepest purpose, wisdom, ethics, spiritual intuition and compassion, then each of us becomes a spiritual work of art.

And yet, the aesthetic experience, however profound, may not be sufficient for developing a constant, mature and fully actualized spiritual path. Although it is a powerful component in one's spiritual repertoire, the Way of the Arts, like each of the other archetypal styles, needs to be supported by the knowledge and experience that emerge from the other spiritual styles. Our job is to intentionally discern the right combination of spiritual styles to serve us best as we journey through the mystery of human existence.

We might also find that more than one art form stimulates our need for expression. Just as we are inspired by the works of other artists, we also need to explore different mediums of expression in order to best reveal that which is within us and to share it with others. Here we are fortunate, as there seem to be nearly as many forms of artistic expression as there are different types of people. Thus, it is up to each of us to discover the form of expression that best matches our skill and need for expression, and which touches upon the mysteries we can feel but which are ordinarily unspoken.

Through the arts, we might find a bridge for crossing over into realms of knowing and being that ordinarily lie dormant in our daily lives. For each of us, there is an art form that can help to transport us to a world we might have intuited, but which we have not touched or inhabited. In the magic of the artistic journey, we might encounter an unexpected moment in which we see, hear, taste or touch something that opens up new possibilities for us, or inspires us to live according to our highest ideals. For each of us, there is a work of art that helps us to know the unknowable, to experience that which lies beyond our ken, to become the person we would like to be.

Through the arts, we also encounter beliefs, images, beings, shapes, colors, smells and sounds that take us beyond our comfort zone. Some of these we even find frightening or repulsive. But these are also great opportunities for psychological and spiritual growth. We might find depictions of archetypes that have lain hidden in our unconscious minds and which are thereby released. Through the arts, we find comprehensive expressions of all that it means to be human, all the potentialities for good and evil within us, and the capacities for transcendence that are imbedded in our infinite human potential.

So we can look at art in a variety of interesting and compatible ways. One way is to celebrate the influence that great works of art have had in the formation of our personal spiritual path, and to surround ourselves with these inspirations. Another is to engage a personally meaningful art form to deepen and to express our own spiritual path. Still another might be to apprentice with a teacher of a traditional art form within, say Tibetan Buddhism or Eastern Orthodox Christianity, and to forge a personal practice that aligns with the spiritual styles and questions outlined in the Mandala. By learning a single tradition well, we are better equipped to understand others. For as many successful artists (and spiritual teachers) tell us, it is helpful to have some classical training in at least one tradition as a foundation and a point of departure.

But even if we strive to make our own beliefs and practices conform to those of a teacher or tradition, we are still unique beings with unique habits, propensities and tastes. Whether we like it or not, we can't help but interpret the teachings of others in our own way. Just as the personality of the classical musician is subtly revealed in a prescribed piece or music, our commonly held spiritual beliefs are uniquely expressed by each of us, and it will be the same with our art.

If the Way of the Arts resonates deeply for you, then explore this archetype fully. Seek out artists and artistic expressions that speak to you, console you, inspire you, and challenge you to deepen and expand your own experience of that which you call 'sacred,' 'divine' and 'true.' Engage in and explore your own artistic expression in whatever form it might take in your life. Likewise, the archetypal style of the Artist can be supported by other spiritual paths, such as The Way of Ritual or The Way of the Body. These will help deepen and mature your spiritual experience and help you to apply your spiritual insights in your personal, professional, and communal lives. Your spiritual path will become your own sacred work of art.

THE WAY OF THE ARTS IN BUDDHISM

The Way of the Arts has been central to Buddhism and my own personal experience of Buddhist practice. In the 5th-century B.C.E., the Buddha himself is said to have instructed the palace artist of King Bimbisara to paint the first Wheel of Life, illustrating his central doctrines. Because Buddhist practice is designed to help transform the practitioner into an enlightened Buddha, the Buddhist arts are designed help inspire and focus the mind toward that end.

Generally, the Buddhist arts are created according to a proscribed set of guidelines meant to help the artist and those who experience the art to deepen their spiritual practice. Thus, Buddhist arts are not exactly forms of free expression by the individual artist. Yet, it is possible to discern subtle individual differences in each work of art that demonstrate the individual artist's skill and spiritual insight. Since the Buddhist arts are not isolated from spiritual practice, they inspire and infuse all the other Buddhist spiritual styles with a sublime, spiritually refined aesthetic. This helps the practitioner to integrate all archetypal styles and focus them on the same goal.

This is especially true within the tantric Vajrayana traditions which require the practitioner to engage in detailed visualizations of deities who themselves embody enlightened states of consciousness. By learning to draw and paint these deities, it becomes easier to visualize them in great detail. These visualizations, along with prayer, mantras, mudras, breath control, energy transformation and meditation on wisdom and compassion, help the practitioner to transform into the mind, body and spirit of a Buddha, and to become 'one with' the deity.

In addition to the traditionally proscribed forms of Buddhist art, contemporary Buddhist practitioners might also engage in their own creative art inspired by Buddhist imagery, wisdom and compassion. The creative artwork of a modern Buddhist might also provide a vehicle for a tranquil, single-pointed focus and meditative insight, expressing a truth that transcends the mundane desires, anxieties and emotions of daily life. In this way, by employing the archetypal style of the arts, artists can deepen their own realization and, in turn, help others do the same.

THE WAY OF THE ARTS IN MY OWN LIFE

Although I have been a filmmaker and can play a few musical instruments, I have never really thought of myself as an artist. Nevertheless, I have good friends who are, and when we talk about work together, I see that the creative process is much the same in all fields. While they create paintings, sculptures, songs and dances, I create books, films, web-sites, curricula and spiritual programs. There is a product to our various forms of creative work and these products are an expression of a uniquely personal synthesis. Thus, I have come to redefine 'artistic activity' for myself.

But with regard to the more traditional arts, I once had the profound experience of collaborating on a work of visual art—the Spiritual Paths Mandala. For those of you who are not familiar with the term, a *mandala* is a geometric design that symbolizes a sacred body of spiritual teachings and practices. It provides a visual and mnemonic aid for remembering a complex system and is often coupled with a verbal *mantra* that helps the practitioner to attain a specific state of consciousness. It's colors and designs are usually beautiful, providing an all-encompassing aesthetic experience for a body of spiritual knowledge and practice.

In my own Buddhist training, I have visualized various mandalas and chanted specific mantras and prayers in order to experience the states of consciousness they are designed to evoke. But while the term *mandala* comes primarily from the Indian traditions of esoteric Buddhism and Hinduism, similar geometric patterns can be found in a variety of spiritual cultures around the world, and the concept and use of mandalas has even become an important part of Jungian psychology.

The visual representation of the Spiritual Paths Mandala is meant to convey an aesthetic of beauty, mystery and antiquity, and to help a practitioner recognize his or her innate spiritual styles and questions and organize them into a mature and meaningful personal path. To create this Mandala, I worked with an artist friend named Sharon Wells. I explained to her my vision of three sets of twelve shapes in the Mandala, the three concentric circles in which the shapes would be drawn, and the white dot in the middle to represent each person's own personal path.

I also shared a dream with Sharon in which I discovered this *mandala* in the ancient ruins of a temple high in the desert-mountains of Central Asia. In the dream, an old and faded *mandala* lay hidden beneath the rubble of an ancient alter that had been destroyed. The geometric patterns in the *mandala* outlined a universal method whereby anyone could create their own personal path. It seemed that this 'ancient temple' lay near the trade routes that connected the cultures of China, India, Egypt, Mesopotamia and Greece. It was a vibrant center of intellectual and spiritual activity where people of all cultures could share their beliefs, practices and experiences. It was a hub of synthesis and expansion of the human potential beyond the ideological confines of remote regions of the world.

The temple in my dream had been destroyed by a king of a neighboring kingdom who had allied with the priests of a religion that believed in a single Universal Ruler-God. The king and his priests wanted everyone in the kingdom to believe only in this God so the people could be more easily governed and live in peace. To solidify their power, these priests proclaimed the king a divine incarnation of the Ruler-God and themselves middlemen between God and the people. Thus, they enacted complex rituals and initiations to please the Ruler-God, to beseech him to bestow peace, good health and prosperity on the people. Therefore, the ordinary people needed to obey both the king and the priests in order to receive the blessings of the Ruler-God.

Since the spirit this temple and its symbolic *mandala* were diametrically opposed to the ideologies of the king and priests, they conspired to destroy the temple. They could not allow for the possibility of an ideology that celebrated spiritual diversity, individual choice and multiple spiritual styles. The *mandala* of the temple was the symbol of this radical ideology, so it also had to be destroyed.**

Over a period of weeks, I explained the details of this dream to Sharon and she drew the shapes for me and colored them with watercolors. The *mandala* she had created was the artistic expression of my own vision—an expression of my own internal yearnings to know, to share this knowledge with others, and to help others discover their own paths. Later, the watercolor image was scanned and took on a slightly different hue, but it still conveyed the beauty and mystery of the original vision. Someday, I hope to see it re-created in stained-glass with the sun filtering through it, illuminating all the world's spiritual styles, questions and traditions.

---

* A fuller account of this dream-vision can be found in the Appendices. This mandala will also become a spherical, online three-dimensional interface, guiding each individual on their 'hero's journey' to create their own spiritual path and to serve others.

"THE KINESTHETE"
THE WAY OF THE BODY

*The Kinesthete uses physical movement as
a primary mode of learning, and experiences
subtle emotional and spiritual states of
consciousness in various parts of their body.*

Does your need for physical activity make it difficult for
you to sit still?

Do you like to explore and express your spiritual
insights through movement?

Do you feel subtle emotional and spiritual states
through your body?

THE KINESTHETE takes pleasure and finds satisfaction in physical
movement and 'listening to the body.' But when a kinesthetic
or somatic learner becomes physically inactive, they can easily
lose emotional balance and mental sharpness, and thus also lose
confidence and begin to suffer from stress.

If your style is the Way of the Body, you learn and practice
spirituality physically, kinesthetically or somatically. You may find
it difficult to sit still through long periods of meditation, prayer,
study or ritual. You may be drawn to Yoga, Tai Chi, Chi Gong, or
physical labor, walking, running, climbing, cooking, serving tea, or
eating. You might even find that the focus of physical exercise helps
you achieve a single-pointed, tranquil, endorphin-driven bliss, or
that your greatest epiphanies arise when your body is engaged in
just the right form of movement.

If this is true for you, then your job is to combine your prayers,
mantras, visualizations, rituals and meditations with physical
movement. Physical activity can help you calm your thoughts
and emotions and engage in the complimentary mental activities

that help us to be receptive to a sacred or otherwise profound experience.

But the Way of the Body entails more than physical activity. It can also connote a more subtle and refined somatic sensitivity to emotions, stress, spiritual epiphanies and the psychological states that can arise in response to relationships with other people and our physical environment. The kinesthete often learns about subtle mental and spiritual states through the body, being sensitive to the subtle physical sensations that reveal inner emotion or resonance. A certain feeling in your stomach or chest might awaken you to some truth or warn you that something is 'not right.' A pain in your back may alert you to an unresolved emotional issue. A quickening of your pulse may alert you to the onset of stress and the need to take remedial action. Indeed, the growing discipline of Somatic Psychology is based on the recognition of this intimate connection between subtle physical and mental states.

Spiritual traditions have sometimes disregarded the body and material existence. But the physical body is inextricably intertwined with our thoughts, sensory perceptions, awareness, sensations, feelings, memories and consciousness. The boundaries between mind, body and spirit are so porous that it is impossible to discern an absolute dividing-line between them. Therefore, spiritual traditions often regard the body as the visible manifestation of the eternal mind and spirit that live on after death. On the other hand, scientists have sometimes treated mind, body and spirit as separate and disconnected from one another, or have asserted that spirit is simply a figment of the imagination, and that all mental functions are simply products of the brain and nervous system. According to these views, mind and spirit cannot survive the death of the body.

However we choose to regard the connection between body, mind and spirit, it is clear that they are causally connected. The health of the body is related to the health of the mind. Physical ailments like high blood pressure, headaches, back pain and skin rashes are often caused by stress and emotional turmoil. Likewise, a relaxed and healthy body can result in a calm, loving and forgiving state of mind. Similarly, the quality of our consciousness depends greatly on how we treat and utilize our bodies. Since our mental health and happiness is related to the health of our bodies, it is crucially important that we provide them with good food, exercise, cleanliness, clothing and shelter.

THE WAY OF THE BODY IN BUDDHISM

While living and studying in the monastery, I was content to let the physical side of my nature take a rest. Days were spent reading, translating, studying with my teacher, attending rituals and meditating. I became immersed in the mental and meditative forms of Buddhist study and practice. And yet, the Way of the Body was present throughout the monastery. There were monks who specialized in constructing and repairing the monastery's buildings, tending the fields, cooking and cleaning. And, as they carried-out these activities, they often continued the internal focus of their meditations, prayers and mantras. They didn't leave their spiritual practice in the temple or on the meditation cushion; it was always present in the background of their minds, and in their interactions with others.

There was also the physical activity of daily debates, often pursued vigorously by the monks in their teens and early twenties. The debates tested their recall of scriptural passages and their ability to argue various interpretations of these passages by great sages. But making one's point and challenging an argument was also accompanied by movements and prescribed gestures that mimicked the physical combat of Tibet's pre-Buddhist culture. Physical contact during debates was not uncommon, as monks would sometimes shove each other out of the way if they thought their argument was stronger. In the monastic setting, this was simply a good-natured and boisterous outlet for young men who lived an otherwise sedentary life of study and meditation.

There are also a variety of meditative practices that focus on the body in Buddhism. These generally begin with tranquil breathing as a way to calm and interiorize the mind. They often focus on the impermanence of the body and the futility of relying on it as a sustainable source of happiness. These meditations begin with the Four Mindfulness Meditations *(Satipatthana),* which include: Mindfulness of Body, Mindfulness of Sensations, Mindfulness of Mind and Mindfulness of Mental Objects. Of these four, meditative focus on the body and sensations are especially useful for extroverts, while meditative focus on the mind and mental objects can be more helpful to those who are introverts. Again, we can see how individual personality and learning styles are factored into traditional Buddhist education and practice.

The Buddhist Way of the Body regards the human form as both an objectofmeditationandasavehiclefortransformation.Mindfulness meditations on the body help us to be conscious of how our state of mind is generally under the control of bodily sensations. With each waking moment, our eyes, ears, nose, tongue and skin are reporting sensations to the brain for processing. Our muscles, organs and nerves are constantly at work relaying sensory data to the brain. It is no wonder that our minds are constantly busy and that we have a difficult time becoming calm, focused and free from the anxieties of physical health and well-being.

Therefore, the Way of the Body in Buddhism begins with our perspective about the impermanent nature and inevitable health challenges of the body. Mentally, we learn to step back and to observe our sensations, rather than obsessively reacting to them from one moment to the next. We suspend our instinctive reactions to external stimuli and the momentary painful and pleasurable bodily sensations they create. We do so based on an understanding that pleasant external stimuli and sensations cannot create lasting happiness, and that unpleasant stimuli and sensations do not have intrinsic power to cause lasting sadness. We replace the autonomic chain of conditioned mental and physical responses with an internal perspective that perceives the interdependent chain of causation surrounding every stimulus and response. The result is a state of tranquil observation wherein we can best discern how to respond with empathy, and in the interest of both ourselves and those around us.

In this way, the body becomes the vehicle for transforming ourselves into the being we most want to become. This is true whether we are exercising, cooking, cleaning, walking or making love. Literally, every physical activity can become a spiritual Way of the Body.

THE WAY OF THE BODY IN MY OWN LIFE

As I look back, I now see that, alongside my very active physical nature, there was always a contemplative part of me longing for expression. For many years, my contemplative search for meaning was overwhelmed by my focus on athletics and physical pleasure. In other words, my kinesthetic spiritual style and my meditative spiritual style were not working in harmony with each other.

In my youth, sports were the major obsession of my life. I excelled in athletics generally, and was an **All-American basketball player in high school and** later went on to play at the University of Iowa. But, being an athlete, I was also stereotyped as someone without much intellectual ability. Consequently, I lost confidence in my capacity to excel academically. I also lost touch with my internal self-validation system. Athletic competition became the primary measure of my self worth. When I won, I felt good; when I lost, I was unhappy.

Even though I felt good about the recognition I received for being a 'good athlete,' and often enjoyed that role, my inner questions did not disappear and contentment continued to evade me. At the end of my competitive athletic career, I learned that I was not alone. Other athletes told me about their own dissatisfaction with the roles society had forced them to play because of their physical abilities. They felt they were the targets of an obsessive focus on sports by their coaches, the fans, and the schools for whom they had once competed. Once they had completed their competitive careers, they felt used by the colleges and teams for which they had played. They were praised when they did well and booed when they did poorly. Their studies often suffered. Unknowingly, young athletes are often manipulated to provide the fans with a psychological release for their own anger and frustration, to become surrogate warriors helping to diffuse societal violence. We were often entertainment, a conversation piece and pawns for college student recruitment and alumni fundraising. These roles might be acceptable for a well-paid professional, but many former athletes, on reflection, think of these roles as being unfairly forced on young people who are unwitting pawns in a larger societal drama.

Even so, I did not give up on my body as a potential source of happiness and fulfillment after my basketball career was over. I was young and healthy and bred to be a pleasure seeker. On the positive side, I changed the focus of much of my physical activity. I became an avid skier and backpacker. I hitchhiked around the world, finally free to leave competitive athletics behind me. In nature, I was led back into a sense of awe before the magic and mystery of life and generally felt healthier and more balanced. There was a primordial connection with the mountain streams, the flowers, the trees, the towering peaks, the seasons, the fresh air and sunlight unimpeded by urban pollution. Gradually, my love of nature began to supplant my need to seek happiness through physical prowess.

Living in Aspen, surrounded by the peaks of the Rocky Mountains, seemed like heaven on earth. Aspen, in the late 1960s and early 70s, combined a pristine natural setting with sublime artistic and cultural activities. Thus, it attracted hundreds of young men and women like myself, fleeing the staid, restrictive lives of our parents. We were rejecting the lives we were brought up to lead; the idea of working hard for forty years only to enjoy a few years of retirement seemed preposterous. We were determined to enjoy life while we were still young and full of energy, to enjoy our bodies to the fullest, rejecting all the taboos we were raised to revere. "Have dessert first" was our motto.

Then one day an Indian Yogi appeared in Aspen. His message was that ultimate happiness could not be achieved through physical pleasure alone. The body, he taught, was a temple containing subtle spiritual energies that could be tapped by proper physical exercise and breathing. He said that physical, mental and spiritual health depended on the free flow and harmonious balance of these internal energies. Once these were properly harmonized, our mind and spirit could attain their full enlightened potential and a state of everlasting bliss. Body, mind and spirit, he explained, were inextricably intertwined. Physical health depended on a healthy mind and actualization of the spiritual elements of our existence. Spiritual actualization also required proper treatment of our bodies, proper breathing, and exercise.

But even before he arrived, some of us were already beginning to question the promise of happiness through sexual freedom and mountain sports. We were having lots of fun, but we still lacked contentment and a deeper sense of happiness. For me, there remained an inner longing for something more enduring than random romance and fun in nature, so the Yogi's message sounded appealing to me. I began to take the idea seriously that true happiness could be found through a more refined use of my body, that my body could actually lead me into the hidden mysteries of my mind and spirit, and to the answers to my deepest questions.

On a purely physical level, I found that Yoga kept my body limber and healthy. And the diet prescribed by the Yogi—consisting of rice and vegetables, rather than the meat and dairy products that dominated American food habits at the time—kept my mind sharp. Relaxing and invigorating chants replaced the structured church music of my childhood and the rock-'n-roll of my youth. I practiced new ways of breathing deeply into the whole of my body, replacing the quick, shallow breathing I had learned in sports. A non-violent reverence for all life replaced the myth that humans had a divine right to thoughtlessly kill animals and abuse the earth. Simple living replaced the myth that 'more is better.'

This Yogi personified a broader societal phenomena in America which saw the influx of Hindu, Buddhist and Taoist ideologies into the western world. This new movement led to the revival of contemplative and mystical practices within Christianity, Judaism and Islam as well. The yogic practices of India taught us that our bodies could become sacred vehicles for a more profound and fulfilling life than the one offered us by sports, 'sex, drugs and rock-'n-roll.' It taught us that our consciousness was eternal, that its relative states of happiness or misery actually depend on the quality of our thoughts and the kindness of our actions. It taught us that consciousness is not merely a physiological phenomenon, but infinitely expandable and capable of unity with the source of all existence. Through Yoga our bodies could become instruments for new possibilities of existence.

My first experiences with Yoga shifted my perspective dramatically and opened a new universe of possibilities for me. I began to feel a shift in my own consciousness and an awakening of deeper potential. Perhaps most importantly, I began to see how my body could help to lead me to the answers to my most pressing questions, questions that had been effectively snuffed-out by the society in which I was raised. This realization led me to experiment with other forms of body-practice like Tai Chi, Chi Gong, meditative walking, and Sufi *dhikr*. I began to see how a mature, fully developed spiritual practice could include and be enhanced by the use of the body, especially by people who are natural kinesthetic learners, for whom the body *must* play a central role in their general education. Since kinesthetic propensities vary from person to person, the adventure is to find the right practices for you.

The past 40 years have witnessed amazing changes in the world and the availability of different body disciplines. Today, practices like Yoga have become almost commonplace; but sadly, we are loosing the spiritual intent and content envisioned by its founders. It has been co-opted by western lifestyle-merchants, western ideas of physical fitness, and even the western medical establishment. Clearly, Yoga in the western model is still helping to reduce stress, promote physical health, and in some small measure does continue to emphasize the spiritual dimensions of practice; but the greatest gifts of Yoga and other profound spirit-body disciplines remain largely unopened by many practitioners and the culture-at-large.

"THE MEDITATOR" OR "CONTEMPLATIVE"
THE WAYS OF CONTEMPLATION
& MEDITATION

The Contemplative or Meditator
is drawn to quiet and solitary introspection
and seeks to discover the truth within or through
communion with the numinous.

Do you long for inner tranquility, focus and insight?

Are you comfortable spending considerable time alone in silence?

Are you called to discover truth and meaning through deep introspection?

THE CONTEMPLATIVE enjoys being alone and absorbed in his or her own thoughts, sometimes for minutes, sometimes for hours or even days. It is a manifestation of that aspect of our consciousness that enjoys observing the world around us and reflecting on the truths revealed through our life-experience, or the wisdom of the world's great philosophers, scientists and spiritual teachers.

The terms contemplation and meditation are defined differently among various spiritual traditions, so I will offer the following definitions so that we are all on the same page.

Contemplation generally refers to thinking deeply and thoroughly. From a spiritual perspective, it refers to a state of consciousness that lies at the border between pure, non-conceptual meditative insight and the conceptual mind that seeks to name and define ineffable spiritual experience. It is characterized by tranquil concentration and profound observation of both the conceptual and the meditative mind. Contemplation is the state of consciousness through which we travel back and forth between the sacred and the secular, the divine and the worldly.

Meditation, on the other hand, has a slightly different connotation. It refers to a wide variety of practices that bring the mind into a state of focused tranquility and profound insight. Meditation enables the mind to become tranquil, one-pointed, blissful and absorbed in a non-conceptual focus on the Ultimate Reality, however that is defined within a spiritual tradition. Often, meditation is described as a 'non-dual,' because in its state of absorption there is no distinction between the subjective and objective elements that occur in normal perception.

In Buddhism, meditation is usually divided into two types: *shamatha* and *vipashyana*. *Shamatha* is a disciplined mental state of one-pointed focus and tranquility that can observe and pacify extraneous mental and sensory distractions. *Vipasyana* is the meditative capacity that utilizes the tranquil, focused mind to gain direct insight into the absolute nature of reality. In Hindu meditation, in the Vedanta tradition, for example, the separate self *(atman)* of the meditator is said to be unified with the universal creator *(Brahman)*.

The Contemplative seeks fulfillment through such solitary and internal spiritual methods as meditation, prayer, breathing, mantra, silence, reflection on sacred writings, disciplined observation and control of the mind, and purposeful cultivation of virtuous thoughts, emotions, words and deeds. Contemplation can occur anywhere and in any situation. Most importantly, contemplation and meditation lead us to the spiritual essence of our being and, for some traditions, unity and oneness with a divine or universal consciousness.

Contemplation and meditation can lead us to quietly concentrate without distraction on a sound, sight or feeling, a taste, smell, intellectual concept, or non-sensory mental object, like a deity, an ethical ideal, emptiness, oneness or compassion. Deep meditation and contemplation generally require careful cultivation and training, as they are difficult to sustain and can have a deep and lasting effect on our states of mind.

Modern neuroscientists have confirmed the power of meditation by observing the places in the brain that are affected by one-pointed, tranquil meditation. They can now chart the profound differences between meditative and non-meditative states of mind. Moreover, scientists have developed experimental protocols that prove the beneficial, healthy effects of meditation on the condition of the body. These scientific studies are validating the psychological and physical health benefits reported by meditators whose traditions go back thousands of years.

Nevertheless, we often tend to overemphasize and romanticize the peaceful solitude of contemplation and meditation. The difficult truth is that meditation can also lead us into the shadows of our unconscious mind, revealing aspects of ourselves that lay hidden behind the sensory stimulation and busyness of our everyday lives. For well-trained practitioners, meditation can be a powerful psychoanalytic tool for profound healing. But without proper training and consultation with a qualified teacher, meditation can often result in unintended psychological discoveries that can be difficult to process.

One of the practical advantages of a mature practice of meditation and contemplation is that it can be done anywhere and at any time. It doesn't necessarily have to be practiced exclusively while sitting alone for long periods in silence. It can also be practiced while walking, lying down or listening to music, while immersed in nature or engaged in such physical activities as swimming, cycling, running, Tai Chi or Yoga. It can provide unsurpassed calm and healing power in times of injury and crisis. While dying, meditation enables us to pass from this life to the next and, according to Hindu and Buddhist teachings, profoundly influence the quality of our next incarnation.

But successful meditation also requires the support of the other spiritual and archetypal styles. For example, without love and compassion, meditation can devolve into a narcissistic endeavor purely for self-benefit. Self-absorbed meditation might have some temporary personal benefit, but the long-term benefits depend on a universal empathy and a vow to help relieve the suffering of others.

THE WAY OF CONTEMPLATION & MEDITATION IN MY OWN LIFE

When I first met the Dalai Lama in 1970, I was looking for answers, yearning for a spiritual foundation and a life-purpose. I was young, energetic, confident . . . and so was he! The major difference, of course, was that he had been rigorously trained from his youth in the teachings and practices of Buddhism, and was now the exiled leader of over a hundred thousand Tibetan Buddhist refugees in India. And yet, amidst the tragedy of exile and his own awesome responsibilities to preserve his religion and culture from extinction, he exuded an infectious enthusiasm, optimism and humor. When I asked how he could possibly maintain this state of mind, he pointed to his daily practice of meditation. When I expressed an interest in learning meditation, he appointed one of his teachers, Geshe Rabten, to get me started.

Geshe Rabten was then living in a small hut, high in the foothills of the Himalayas above Dharamasala, India. Every other day, accompanied by his student and translator, Gonsar Tulku, I would walk up the mountain for instruction. On our first meeting, he asked me why I wanted to study Buddhism, and I told him it was because I wanted to understand the nature of the mind. "To understand the nature of the mind," he said, "you must learn to meditate." That was the beginning of over forty years of meditation practice.

Buddhism, of course, is best known for meditation, and its most enduring image is the Buddha seated in the lotus posture, meditating under the Bodhi Tree during his enlightenment experience. People sometimes ask, what is he actually doing during this meditation? Tradition tells us that it was during this meditation that the Buddha eliminated the mental obstacles that prevented him from perceiving directly and instantaneously the true nature of existence, as well as the totality of existence past, present and future. His purpose for meditating was to achieve Enlightenment in order to liberate all beings from suffering. He had concluded that his own personal wisdom, happiness and freedom required him to work first and foremost for the liberation of others. In short, selfishness leads to misery, and altruism to happiness. Meditation is a necessary condition for achieving sustainable happiness for both ourselves and others. It unlocks the natural capacity of our mind to be enlightened, liberated and fully capable of helping others to do the same.

The Buddha had trained long and hard for this moment with India's greatest living teachers. In his enlightenment quest, he overcame attachment to worldly pleasures because he knew that these could not lead to lasting happiness or liberation from suffering. In his meditation, he cultivated a constant, focused equanimity called *shamatha*. With that as a foundation, he cultivated a wisdom called *vipashyana* that directly perceived the interdependence of all things, and the myriad causal factors underlying every instant in time.

These meditations enabled him to intuit the inner psychological conditions of his students and to provide them with the specific instructions they needed. Through visualization, mantra practice and ritual, he transformed himself into the embodiment of transcendent wisdom, compassion, bliss, omniscience and omnipotence.

Likewise, countless Buddhist practitioners for the past two thousand five hundred years have attempted to cultivate the capacities of a Buddha, and to become liberated and enlightened through these same meditations. So I felt I was in safe hands learning to meditate from the Dalai Lama and Geshe Rabten, who were both so meticulously trained in this ancient tradition.

After decades of Buddhist meditation, I came to the realization that I had to take personal responsibility for my practice, and not depend solely on the literal instructions of my teachers and the Buddhist texts. This realization came after working closely with mature meditation teachers from various traditions, as I began to see the common processes and experiences of meditation in Christianity, Judaism, Hinduism, Islam, Buddhism and Taoism. In the end, my experience with other meditators led to the development of my book, *InterSpiritual Meditation*, which draws on the shared processes within all these traditions and encapsulates the practices I have learned in Buddhism.

So whether or not you consider yourself a meditator, you might begin to explore the marvelous variety of contemplative practices that are most congenial to your primary archetypal spiritual style.

"THE DEVOTEE"
THE WAY OF DEVOTION

The Devotee is naturally loyal and
lovingly committed to a job, a relationship,
a set of principles, a way of life, a daily routine,
a religious teacher, a spiritual tradition or a life-goal.

Are you more prone to faith than skepticism?

Are you are naturally loyal to a job, a person or a community?

Do you yearn to be dedicated to a greater cause or higher principle?

Do you long to be committed to a spiritual teaching, teacher or higher power?

MANY OF OUR MOST important life-goals are virtually impossible to achieve without commitment and dedication. Whether the goal lies in the fields of athletics, academics, the arts, society or spirituality, we need to be devoted to our objective, to our teacher, and even to the founder of the tradition of our teacher. Why? Because, in practical terms, devotion helps us to be steady, consistent and determined. Simply put, devotion is a practical psychological tool for accomplishing any life-goal.

We naturally devote ourselves to the things we think will make us happy. But, during the course of our lives, we are often disillusioned because the objects of our devotion don't always bring us happiness. When this happens, we shouldn't blame devotion, but rather, the false hopes and dreams we projected onto the object, person, goal or idea to which we were devoted.

And yet, there are good reasons for being leery of spiritual devotion. Too often we have seen how so-called spiritual teachers have abused devotees desperate for spiritual bliss and enlightenment. Therefore, we must carefully examine the qualities of potential teachers before becoming devoted to them and their teachings. An old Hindu maxim tells us, "Since it is the disciple who must judge the *guru*-ness of the *guru,* it is the disciple who is the *guru* of the *guru.*"

Thus, for devotion to be effective, it should be accompanied by other spiritual styles, such as the Way of Reason; for it is up to us to discern what is worthy of our devotion. Impetuous devotion often leads to heartbreak. When it comes to spirituality, devotion is just one of a number of necessary conditions for success. Devotion needs to be accompanied by intelligence, prayer, ritual and compassionate interaction with fellow beings. Devotion alone may not be sufficient for spiritual awakening and transformation.

As an example, the Buddha advised his students to test a teacher's words just as a goldsmith tests for real gold—through tasting, rubbing, cutting and burning. He advised us not to be convinced by the personality of a teacher, but by his or her example—not just by the teacher's example, but by his or her words—and not just by the literal meaning of the words, but by the implicit and deeper meanings of the words. That is to say, he advised students to evaluate the teacher critically before making a commitment, and to make sure that the teacher is 'walking the talk' before following in his or her footsteps.

Although some people are especially predisposed to devotion, we all have devotional qualities. We all have a natural tendency to be dedicated to a particular goal or to emulate a certain person. Our devotional tendencies begin in childhood. For example, some children are attracted to the idea of becoming doctors. The mind forms a composite image of 'a doctor' with certain desirable attributes which, over time, becomes an object of devotion. Through the strength of this devotion, some are able to endure the many years of training it takes to obtain a medical degree and become a doctor. Similarly, we have the potential to adapt ourselves to other images that match our highest spiritual aspirations. Devotion is essential for getting us there, and it is up to us to choose wisely and evaluate that to which we will become devoted.

When it comes to spiritual practice, the Devotee naturally seeks a teacher, a divine principal or life-purpose to believe in. The trouble arises when the Devotee does not have something in which they wholeheartedly believe. In this case, the Devotee is at a loss.

Therefore, the first step is to consciously set out on a journey to discover the principal or purpose that is most compatible with one's own life-experience and one's own internal judgment. In essence, this is the hero's journey—to find meaning and a purpose to fulfill one's devotional predisposition.

This exploration may lead a person to study the world's religions and philosophies, to talk with wisdom-holders from various traditions, to experiment with one or more contemplative practices, or to utilize the gifts of their other archetypal styles in service of their primary style of devotion. A person might use intellectual judgment to define an object of devotion suitable for their own temperament and overall set of beliefs. Once the object of devotion is clearly defined, their psychological tension and imbalance will disappear. They will be on their way to establishing a personal spiritual path. Gradually, they will also bring all their other 'Ways' into harmony, having a daily ritual to help them focus on and achieve the benefits of such devotion. In this manner, they build maturity, balance and consistency in their spiritual life.

THE WAY OF DEVOTION IN BUDDHISM AND MY OWN LIFE

By the time I reached my teens, I had acquired an aversion to religious devotion. Devotion seemed to require 'blind faith' and a belief unsubstantiated by logic and empirical science. Worse, preachers who demanded the devotion of their congregations often seemed to take advantage of them for their own personal gain, and religious fanatics committed acts of violence against people who were devoted to another faith. Thus, it seemed to me that devotion conveyed a sense of entitlement and moral superiority, often with horrific results.

This early aversion even carried over into my study and practice of Buddhism. I puzzled over why so many Buddhists in Asia engaged in devotional prayers and rituals. Egotistically, I concluded that my interest in philosophy and meditation were somehow 'higher' and 'more sophisticated' forms of practice, that prayers were simply for folks who didn't have the same capacity or time to spend in these pursuits. And yet, I couldn't ignore the fact that my own brilliant and accomplished teachers often spent hours practicing devotional rituals and prayers. So I began to ask my teachers why they did these devotional practices. The answers

I received were very practical, and soon, a practice of devotion began to make sense to me.

Devotion, they explained, is simply a mental trait that underlies many of our life-pursuits. The completion of difficult tasks requires a determination, dedication and commitment synonymous with devotion. Devotion, they said, begins with a clear mental image of that object toward which we would strive. They pointed to the example of children who naturally form images of the kinds of doctors, nurses, policemen, firemen and athletes they would wish to become; these images provide them with tangible goals, rather than abstract notions, as I have already pointed-out.

Similarly, Buddhist devotional images are used to focus our minds on the qualities these images represent. The Buddha, for example, is represented in a variety of forms that illustrate his meditation, enlightenment, compassion, wisdom and healing powers. These images often contain multiple heads, arms and hands, holding objects that represent the virtuous qualities the Buddha has achieved. Colorful geometric mandalas likewise illustrate the divine abodes of representational, deity-like beings and the meditative practices necessary to achieve their higher states of mind. Sacred letters provide the foundation for chants that lead the mind to these goals. Ritual objects include the bell that represents the wisdom and the *vajra,* or lightning-bolt, that represents the compassionate methods required for becoming a Buddha. All these objects provide a focus for achieving the qualities of mind embodied by the Buddha.

Transforming ourselves from ordinary beings into the mind and body of a Buddha requires extraordinary commitment to ethical conduct, patience, perseverance and meditation. Devotion, therefore, is simply a matter of necessity and practicality. Devotion isn't required to 'curry favor' with a teacher or deity, because our future rests primarily in our own hands. Although prayers to supernatural beings might be very helpful, there are no beings that can magically transport us to *nirvana* and enlightenment simply because we are devoted to them. Thus, the Way of Devotion is very important because it is the internal state of mind that keeps us focused on our highest goals and aspirations. It is a necessary condition for Nirvana, Enlightenment and Buddhahood.

With devotion comes other mental attributes that help propel us along our transformative journey. For example, Buddhist practices often include offerings to the teacher and the teachings as symbols of our commitment. Just as we offer our time and resources to the worldly goals to which we are devoted, a Buddhist offers these to the achievement of their highest spiritual goals. Similarly, a Buddhist might pray to the Buddha for help and guidance with the understanding that prayer activates a deep connection and resonance with the sacred. Prayer awakens the potential for enlightenment that resides hidden beneath the layers of our emotions and concepts.

This practical way of understanding devotion makes sense to me. In spite of my early aversion to devotional practice, I slowly learned to incorporate devotional elements into my overall Buddhist practice.

"THE DREAMER"
THE WAY OF IMAGINATION

The Dreamer naturally dwells in
the imaginary awareness of possibility,
intrigued by images arising from the
limitless depths of consciousness.

Do you have vivid and memorable dreams?

Are you drawn to spiritual symbols, icons and imagery?

Are you naturally interested in mythological stories and beings?

Have you had a rich and vivid imagination since childhood?

WHEN YOU REALLY THINK about it, everything we do involves imagination. This is true both when we are awake and when we are asleep. Imagination is a part of every perception and cognition—the food we choose for breakfast, the thoughts we think, the words we speak, the scents we smell, the forms we feel, and the sounds we hear. Indeed, consciousness itself is a virtual imagination engine that constantly creates the images that condition every aspect of our existence. Therefore, understanding and refining our imaginal capacity is important for shaping our spiritual path.

Every object of conception and perception is associated with the name of a category, and that name and category are themselves associated with a mental image that corresponds to the external thing associated with that category. For example, our visual perception of an apple tree is only fully cognized when our mind associates it with the category of tree and the subcategory of apple tree. In order to fully recognize the tree, the visual perception must match up with an internal category, image and name.

Similarly, our future states of being are also products of our internal categories, names and images. As babies, our minds gradually associate sensory perceptions with words, categories and generic images. Each day, our ability to speak and to ask for the things we want and need gradually evolves. As children, we begin to recognize the occupations of adults by their categorical names, like doctor, nurse, mother, father, lawyer, fireman, policeman, banker, priest and teacher. These categories are then associated with images of, say, your first grade teacher and the way she dresses, talks and acts. If you were inspired by her in those years, your own career aspirations may have been shaped by these images from childhood.

As our future aspirations are conditioned by these familiar categories, along with the images and names we have for each of them, we could say that our past, present and future are all products of imagination. As we intentionally formulate our careers, life-goals and relationships, our challenge is to marry a specific category and a particular image with our own natural styles of learning and being.

Our internal images of human expression and human possibility are related to various personality types found among human beings everywhere, and represent the kinds of worldly and spiritual beings we might become. Although largely hidden from our everyday awareness, they nevertheless exert a powerful influence on our preferences, the choices we make, and even our identities. They are the archetypes that underlie our ways of thinking, feeling, being and becoming.

The word archetype comes from both Latin and Greek, and refers to the 'original model,' 'form,' or 'mold' from which other less perfect copies are made. For the depth psychologist, Carl Jung, the archetypes of human existence reside in the unconscious mind, from whence they exert a powerful influence on our goals, thoughts and actions. Jung believed the archetypes of an individual's unconscious mind are somehow connected within a universal consciousness in which the consciousness of all human beings are interrelated.

This notion of archetypes is also echoed in the philosophy of Plato, who attempted to show that all earthly categories and sensory perceptions are like shadows of the real categories which exist in another sphere altogether. In the Socratic dialogues, he attempted to prove that forms (including archetypes and categories) are the foundation for all our perceptions.

Archetypes of remarkable similarity are found in myths throughout the world. The characters in myths personify the possibilities of our own being and help us to recognize, for instance, the consequences of allowing certain negative traits within us to dominate our behavior without, say, the moderating influences of other archetypal traits associated with wisdom and compassion. They also help us see the human condition more clearly and provide us with models to emulate, if we have sufficient courage and perseverance to do so.

This notion of archetypes is also expressed in such diverse tools as the Enneagram, the Myers-Briggs test, the astrological signs, and the major arcana of the Tarot. Each of these helps us to gain self-knowledge and clarity around our own natural personality traits, how they influence our destinies and our ways of being in relationship with others.

Therefore, as we intentionally set off to create our own spiritual path, it is helpful to examine the archetypal images residing in the background of our minds. This can be done by looking inwardly at the twelve styles of the Spiritual Paths Mandala as archetypal categories of being; each of these is associated with our own internal archetype of the artist, the meditator, the devotee, the dreamer, the lover, the mystic, the hermit, the intellectual, the *mensch*, and the wisdom-keeper. Looked at from this perspective, these twelve styles might be called twelve 'spiritual archetypes.'

In creating our spiritual path, our job is to bring each archetype to the surface of our minds so that we might examine the images and qualities we have unconsciously ascribed to each. Our task is to refine the images we have for each archetype so that they might work harmoniously within us. For example, we might find that our image of the mystic who experiences fantastic visions is in conflict with our image of the intellectual that discounts these visions as irrational and attempts to abolish them. Or, we might find that our image of the meditator is in conflict with our image of the *mensch* who relishes engagement in challenging relationships. We must work out these conflicts so that our images of the different styles become complimentary resources for one another, rather than antagonistic opposites.

The creation of our spiritual path may also be enhanced by

refining our own image of the ideal being we wish to become. This might be a literal, anthropomorphic figure of a saint or a deity, or even a symbol or a *mandala*. Sacred images like these can represent such attributes as wisdom, compassion, bravery, kindness and generosity, and help us to focus our minds on our ultimate spiritual goal.

For some of us, the Way of Imagination might function as our dominant process of transformation. For others, it will provide a supporting role. In either case, it is important that we recognize the power of imagination and find ways to channel it toward our highest spiritual aspirations.

THE WAY OF IMAGINATION IN BUDDHISM AND MY OWN LIFE

On the surface, at least, Imagination would seem to be one of my least developed ways of learning. But I have always had an appreciation for imagination, and as I have gotten older, it has more and more become an important part of my spiritual practice.

In my childhood, imagination had a lot to do with my fears. I remember how I would lay in bed at night with visions of fierce creatures wandering the floor beneath my bed. Thus, I was always careful not to let my hands or feet dangle over the side of the bed for fear of being bitten by little foxes that lay in wait there. To protect me from the foxes, I had my imaginary friends—Poogie and Khaka—with whom I carried on a conversation after saying my nightly prayers. My biggest challenge was always to get from my bed to the steps leading up to the bedroom door and the hallway to the bathroom without being attacked. So, before leaping from my bed to the steps, I would have to make sure that my little protectors would prevent the foxes from nipping at my toes on the way!

Tibetan Buddhism, heavily influenced by the indigenous Bön religion, makes powerful use of the imagination. Tibetan monasteries are filled with sculptures and paintings depicting the life of the Buddha, Buddhist saints, and Buddhist deities, whose physical forms symbolize virtuous qualities like love, compassion, wisdom, power, protection and enlightenment. There are also images of spirit-beings that preside over local valleys, mountains, waters, skies, plants, animals and the earth. Whether these images emerge from actual perceptions of real beings, or from archetypes in our own unconscious minds, the artistic imagination, or a combination of these, no one can say for sure. Nevertheless, they exist and are real in the imagination of those who relate to them; and serious Buddhist practitioners might focus on the images of deities in order to emulate and embody their sacred qualities. This type of imagining can become a powerful tool for inner transformation.

On the surface, this use of the imagination might seem to contradict other Buddhist practices, like emptying the mind of all concepts, memories, emotions, sensations and images, and learning to rest in a non-dual state of emptiness. But once this state of mind is established, the Buddhist meditator enters into another phase of practice wherein the mind cultivates insight regarding the emptiness and interdependence of all phenomena. At this stage, the imagination is active again, attempting to 'see' everything as interdependent and empty of inherent existence. This direct perception of interdependence and emptiness is especially important for meditations on the images of deities who are also understood to be empty of inherent existence.

In Buddhist Tantric meditations, the practitioner visualizes various deities, their qualities and their heavenly abodes in order to radically transform their body, speech, and mind into an enlightened Buddha. These meditations focus on the subtle breath-energy that enlivens the body, and the movement of this energy through the spiritual anatomy of chakras, nadis, and channels that form the subtle structure of the human body. They transform the raw energies of sexual desire, attachment, and even anger, into deity-like bodies that manifest compassionate wisdom for all beings. For example, there are meditative visualizations on various forms: Manjushri, the Bodhisattva of Wisdom; Avalokiteshvara, the Bodhisattva of Compassion; Bhaisajya Guru, the Bodhisattva of Healing; Padmasambhava, a Bodhisattva with magical and psychic Power: and Tara, the Bodhisattva of Love. Associated with each of these meditations are specific rituals, prayers and practices that help the aspirant to cultivate, emulate, and embody these same qualities.

So you can see, the Buddhist Way of Imagination follows proscribed formulas that give rise to specific archetypal images that hasten the transformation of ordinary human beings into Buddhas. In this process, the images that arise in dreams are also reported by a student to the Tantric teacher for analysis. These dream-images help the teacher to discern the student's stage of development and to proscribe specific practices to enhance the student's transformative process.

Thus, the Buddhist Way of Imagination begins with emptying the mind of the tainted projections that preoccupy and imprison it. It continues with analytic insight that directly perceives the interdependence of all phenomena, realizing the capacity of one's own consciousness to be transformed into the wisdom and compassion of a Buddha. It then systematically rebuilds consciousness using techniques of imagination, yogic breath, and energetic transformation to make oneself into a new being that is the personification of these qualities.

Even though the Way of Imagination wasn't initially a primary archetypal style for me, it has become a very important feature of my practice today. Years ago, I was puzzled and resistant to the claims made by the Buddhist Tantric traditions that imaginal practices can speed up our spiritual evolution; but I now see that, with proper training and guidance, these practices are critically important elements of a fully developed spiritual path.

For the Way of Imagination to be effective, however, it needs to be balanced and supported by other archetypal styles, such as Wisdom, Love, Devotion, Meditation, Prayer and Reason. Without these, imagination can lead us down paths that can be psychologically dangerous to ourselves and to others.

"The Lover"
The Way of Love and Compassion

*The Lover naturally experiences
the universality of love and seeks to bring
happiness and relief to the suffering of others.*

Do you have a natural empathy for others?

Do you long to create happiness and eliminate suffering?

Do you have a naturally kind-hearted feeling toward others?

Do you feel embraced by a universal love and compassion greater than yourself?

Love is perhaps the most profound and complex word in the human language. Its varied meanings range from intense liking or desire, to the experience of universal interconnectedness and unconditional empathy with the whole of existence. Love and compassion are at the heart of the world's great spiritual traditions. Love is often said to be synonymous with the divine essence and the well-spring of all life.

When we are in love, we often feel as if we are 'one' with our beloved. There is an irresistible magnetism toward them, and a palpable physical sensation pervades our whole being. We experience a nearly unbreakable force that unites our souls, whether we are together or apart. When we are truly in love with someone, we will do everything we can to protect, nourish and support them. We make their happiness our first priority.

When we are in love spiritually, we experience an undeniable universal interconnectedness, oneness, empathy and compassion for the infinite whole of existence. We instinctively experience love as an all-enveloping cosmic embrace. Love is perceived as a force inseparable from the fundamental impulse of life. We feel ignited by the spark of the divine that infuses the deepest essence of our being. Every cell of our body resonates with the bliss of the divine. We are as a drop of water infused within an infinite ocean. We realize that we are joined inexorably in the web of being and have no choice but to accept our universal responsibility to help remove the causes of suffering of all living things.

The Way of Love and Compassion leads us naturally and unquestionably into the service of others. It is the foundation for spiritual activism, or engaged spirituality. When our motivation is love, then we compassionately engage with everyone in our families, communities, and professional lives. Our lives become living examples of our highest ideals, irrespective of our occupations, relative wealth or social status. Through this altruistic, spiritual love, our compassionate engagement with others becomes an unselfish insurance policy that guarantees our own personal happiness and well-being.

While there are some who are naturally infused and surrounded by the experience of spiritual love, many of us need to be led into it through prayer, contemplation, meditation, ritual or even nature. Of course, it helps greatly to be in the presence of someone who embodies and radiates spiritual love to give us confidence that it is possible, and to help guide us along our path. We cannot achieve spiritual love through will-power alone, for this supreme love will elude our needy, egotistical grasp. It is subtle, delicate, and refined, but once embodied, it is indestructible.

To begin on the Way of Love and Compassion, we need only to develop the honest and sincere wish and intention to be infused and surrounded by it. With intention as the starting point, the path opens up before us and beckons us inexorably to its source.

THE WAY OF LOVE AND COMPASSION IN BUDDHISM

In Buddhism, the archetypal style of Love and Compassion is the foundation for all Buddhist practice and a necessary condition for sustainable health and happiness. The image most commonly associated with this archetypal style is that of Kwan Yin (Sanskrit, *Avalokiteshvara*, Tibetan, *Chenrezig*) who is often depicted with a tear in his or her eye, shed over the suffering of earthly beings. In Tibetan Buddhism, the Dalai Lama is believed to be the incarnation of this compassionate emanation of the Buddha.

The vow of Great Compassion in Mahayana Buddhism seals one's commitment to relieve the suffering of all beings by promising to become an enlightened Buddha; it is only through Enlightenment that we will have the wisdom that truly knows how to help others. This vow is the entry-point to the Path of the Bodhisattva in which we give our word to remain in the world for as long as there are beings who suffer. Remaining in the world, however, does not prohibit our own internal liberation from the causes of suffering; the meditative practices of the Bodhisattva can actually liberate us internally so that we do not suffer while helping those who are. In this way, *nirvana* and Enlightenment are manifested in the here and now, rather than in another transcendent realm where we are mentally and physically separated from ordinary reality.

Great Compassion is fortified by our meditations on interdependence. It is in this meditation that we begin to recognize the natural reciprocity that exists in the universe—how the health and well-being of one being depends on the benevolent thoughts and actions of another. We realize how each of us is enmeshed in an infinite web of interbeing. We learn that narcissistic self-cherishing is actually antithetical to our own self-interest. And yet, in the pure intention of Great Compassion, there is no thought of self-interest. One's own liberation cannot be achieved if that is our primary motivation. Therefore, at the time of taking the Bodhisattva Vow of Great Compassion, our state of mind must be fully altruistic. It is this pure wish that distinguishes it from other forms of altruism. Having taken the vow, the purpose of spiritual practice is to cultivate the wisdom and methods that can actually relieve the suffering of others. Every meditation, ritual and action in the world is infused by this intention.

The reality of our lives, however, is that we are often not feeling love and compassion for others. Therefore, within Buddhism, there are meditations, visualizations and prayers to help us engender love and compassion, even when it doesn't arise spontaneously. But, underneath all the practices, there is a foundational quality of being which all spiritual traditions agree on. It is called *empathy*—a state of consciousness in which we truly connect with other sentient beings, heart-to-heart. And in this connection, we naturally and spontaneously do what we can to help others.

But Buddhism also recognizes that Love and Compassion alone, while necessary, may not be sufficient for a fully actualized spiritual path. They too need the support of our other archetypal styles, like Wisdom and Meditative Insight, which can discern the best way to help others along their own spiritual journeys. So, if the archetype of the Lover is natural for you, it might be useful to bring along the archetypes of the *Mensch,* the Intellect and the Sage to help you gain the knowledge and the wisdom through which you can truly help others. On the other hand, if the Way of Love and Compassion are not natural for you, it might be important to find a way to cultivate this archetype as a necessary condition for your own happiness and liberation.

The world's spiritual and philosophical traditions provide a marvelous variety of teachings and methods to help us all embody love and compassion. The adventure is in finding the ones that work the best for you.

THE WAY OF LOVE AND COMPASSION IN MY OWN LIFE

One sunny winter afternoon in the high country above Aspen, Colorado, I was cross-country skiing with a few good friends. It was the 21st of December, and the thin ski tracks along the ground were icy and hard, barely covering the rocks on the ground beneath. Our group ranged in age from six to sixty, and I was bringing up the rear to make sure that the young ones didn't fall too far behind.

As I paused beneath a lovely grove of white Aspen trees, waiting for the youngest to ski ahead of me, I lost my balance and fell on my left hip. It was a silly, simple fall but my left thigh crashed down on a slightly exposed rock causing me immediate, excruciating pain. Lying there, I looked down the trail to see the littlest girl pause and then yell forward to her mother, "Mommy, the big man is lying on the ground, and I don't think he is sleeping!"

An hour later, after a painful rescue by snowmobile and ambulance, the orthopedic surgeon at the hospital confirmed that I had broken my hip and needed immediate surgery. Fortunately, my son Jonathan was arriving that night for the Christmas holidays and was able to help me through. Somehow, we still had a wonderful holiday together.

Six weeks later, I was in Santa Barbara leading a weekend InterSpiritual retreat at La Casa de Maria. It was Saturday morning, and I had already introduced Father Thomas Keating, who spoke the night before, and was about to introduce Rabbi Rami Shapiro when I was stricken by a pain in my chest. It was so sharp that it nearly brought me to my knees. Barely able to breath, I asked a friend, Juliet, to call an ambulance. Before I knew it, I was lying in the emergency room hearing the doctor's diagnosis: "You have a pulmonary embolism—blood clots in your lungs. There are lots of them, and there is a good possibility that one of these will land in the wrong place, and you will die. There is nothing I can do but give you morphine for the pain and blood thinner to try to dissolve the clots." It worked, and three days later, they released me from the hospital.

This was my second run-in with death. A few years earlier, I had been stung by a bee and had actually died. Fortunately, a very talented EMT was able to bring me back to life. This incident compelled me to sell my Internet company, start the Spiritual Paths Foundation, and to begin researching what eventually became the book, *Living Fully, Dying Well*.

A couple of months after the pulmonary embolism diagnosis, I was sitting with Reverend Alan Jones, Dean of the Episcopal cathedral in San Francisco, having a simple lunch in his office. Alan described in great detail his recent experience with Prostate Cancer, during which he decided not to pursue surgery, but to follow the advice of a Chinese physician: a macrobiotic diet, daily yoga and meditation, prayer, and to *"Love your cancer."* When he uttered these words, I suddenly realized that I didn't know that kind of love. How could he love these tiny cells devouring his body? Where would that love come from?

That night, I drove down Highway 1 to the Santa Cruz home of my dear friends and colleagues, the Sufi teachers, Camille and Kabir Helminski. We spent the weekend talking about the love that was central to their tradition of Islam founded by Jalaluddin Rumi. I realized that my very rational approach to Buddhism did not engender the kind of love of which Alan Jones had spoken, and the quality of love described by Rumi. While I felt unconditional love for my children and family, it didn't resonate through every cell of my body, it didn't hold me in its arms, it didn't emerge from a universal source beyond the confines of my own consciousness. Without a greater presence of love, how could I love the bee and blood clots that had nearly killed me?

Because of discussions like these, with colleagues of other traditions, I have become so grateful for the InterSpiritual work of the Spiritual Paths Foundation. For, it is in deep meditation and dialogue with mature spiritual beings of other traditions that we are challenged to go deeper within our own tradition and to develop qualities within ourselves that have been untouched by our own spiritual practice. It is in these moments of personal crisis that the shared wisdom of all spiritual traditions becomes our greatest gift.

"THE MYSTIC"
THE WAY OF THE MYSTIC

The Mystic naturally feels, intuits, communes with
or otherwise experiences the mysteries of the numinous
that lie beyond the boundaries of ordinary human perception.

Have you had unexplainable experiences of the supernatural?

Are you attracted to the possibility of mystical visions and revelations?

Have you had paranormal experiences not mediated by your five senses?

Are you drawn to an unseen mystery that could reveal the ultimate nature of reality?

THERE IS A REMARKABLE SIMILARITY between the spiritual writing of mystics from many of the world's major religions. Remove the names and specific terminology and you'd think they were all members of the same tradition.

The mystical way within us feels, intuits, communicates with or otherwise experiences mysteries beyond ordinary human perception. I use the word "mysteries" because the things a mystic perceives are things that can only be wondered about, guessed at or deduced; they can't be tangibly perceived or shared through the normal senses. Even so, mystical perception is one of the most important ways in which people approach their spirituality.

However, not all mystical experiences are spiritual, and not everyone who is spiritual has mystical experiences. For some, mystical experiences are common; but for many others, they are not. Even if we have had experiences that seem paranormal, we might not be able to discern: (a) if we have mystical powers; (b) if our mysterious experiences like seeing ghosts or premonitions are truly mystical; (c) what to do with and how to interpret experiences which seem mystical; (d) how to judge or trust such experiences when they occur; (e) how to balance the experiences with those of the normal world; (f) how to effectively use these experiences for spiritual realization; or (g) how to integrate these experiences into the normal belief systems of our family, church and society that generally rejects them.

It is not uncommon for us to yearn for such mystical experiences, if only to prove that there is a reality beyond that of our everyday perceptions and that which is validated by science. But a mystical experience doesn't necessarily help us to become a better person or to sustain a spiritual path; indeed, these experiences can often be unsettling and raise more questions than they answer. They are so alien from our ordinary perceptions that the disjunct between the mystical and the ordinary can result in a psychological imbalance. Such an imbalance can often affect a person's relationships with others, leading to isolation and unhappiness.

In an effort to maintain psychological equilibrium, the Mystic might choose to deny or close themselves off from mystical experiences altogether. Or, they might chose to balance the Mystic archetype with other internal spiritual styles, such as the Way of Reason. Using the intellect, it is possible to learn from the scientific literature on paranormal experiences, read works of the great mystics throughout the ages, and talk with other mature mystics who have found a rational justification for these experiences in a combination of scientific and spiritual explanations. In time, it is possible for one to regard the mystical as a healthy feature of human experience and to find out how it fits into the perceptions of everyday reality. After all, these types of experiences are not considered unusual by indigenous cultures throughout the world, and are well-known in nearly every religious tradition.

THE WAY OF THE MYSTIC IN BUDDHISM

Within every religion, there are reports of divinely inspired visions and communications. Depending on the messenger and the receiver, reports of these mystical experiences can produce skepticism and even derisive laughter, or they can engender deep faith in the divine mysteries of religious experience. Buddhism is no exception. Meditation is said to open our capacity to intuitively interact with other beings, even those who are not human. These might include other animal species, as well as spirit beings whose presence among us cannot be seen through our normal modes of perception, like earth spirits, ghosts, protector deities, *devas, dakinis*, ancestors, and emanations of the Buddha.

Buddhist meditation is also said to awaken the capacity of our consciousness to intuit another person's inner thoughts, emotions, and the causes of their mental and physical suffering. Because meditation improves our intuitive capacity, this ability needs to be grounded on a moral commitment to use these intuitive powers wisely and compassionately. For, if they are used for self-serving ends, the personal karmic consequences could be severe. Therefore, these powers are to be balanced with wisdom, compassion, and insight into the true nature of reality.

Buddhism generally does not regard such perceptions as unusual. It recognizes that we live in an infinite universe with infinite possibilities. Similarly, our consciousness has an infinite capacity to expand. But psychic interactions with other beings is not necessarily a sign of positive spiritual transformation in Buddhism. After all, many people all over the world have reported these experiences, and many have used their powers for selfish and malevolent ends. Therefore, it is not the raw mystical, paranormal or psychic experience that is remarkable. Rather, it is our capacity to discern and interpret the value of these experiences, and to use these interactions to help bring happiness and relieve the suffering of others.

The Buddhist Way of the Mystic might emerge naturally from many years of meditation, but it might also be a natural to certain people who do not even have a deep contemplative practice. In any case, it is important that one be tempered by an empathic wisdom, vowing to do no harm, and to use this capacity only to help heal the suffering of others. Therefore, the archetypal Way of the Mystic should also be centered, stabilized and fully actualized with the support of the other styles; preoccupation with mystical experiences is not sufficient for a fully developed spiritual path.

THE WAY OF THE MYSTIC IN MY OWN LIFE

Early on in my practice of meditation, I had reoccurring visions of the Buddha seated in meditation beneath a tree about fifty feet in front of me. Each time I would sit down to meditate, the Buddha seemed to appear before me. This experience helped to calm my mind and inspire me to continue practice. But I wondered if this could this be real, and if so, would the Buddha actually communicate directly with me in my meditation!?

One day, I told my teacher about this, and he neither encouraged or discouraged my curiosity. He only said that every experience has both an objective and a subjective element. Whatever appears before us is somewhat conditioned by our own mental predispositions and internal ways of knowing. Maybe this vision was a projection of the Buddha within, I conjectured. I found my teacher's answer very helpful, especially since it helped put a damper on the ego-inflation that can occur from a mystical vision. For, too often, people rely on a mystical vision as 'proof' that they are progressing on the spiritual journey. Unfortunately, some claim that their mystical experiences give them the authority to become spiritual teachers. Often, these 'teachers' lack the necessary wisdom, compassion and experience to be reliable and trustworthy guides for the devotees they attract. In other words, mystical experiences alone do not make a good spiritual teacher.

Over the years, like many people, I have seen ghosts, heard voices and received insights, and had a number of paranormal experiences. After my sightings of ghosts, my rational mind always tried to discount the experience and seek another explanation. "Maybe it was just the quality of the light and shadows, or a case of blurred vision." But my experiential consciousness would argue back, "No, this experience was completely real!" And so an argument ensued. But, at the very least, these experiences opened my mind to the possibilities that we could experience realities beyond our normal sense perception, realities that could not be rationally confirmed or experientially denied. (Once, many years ago, I even heard an authoritative voice compelling me to finish this book while sitting by a mountain stream! But that is another story.)

After years of meditation, the sharp divisions between ordinary and extraordinary experiences have softened. I have learned that the paranormal for one person can be normal for another. And if mystical experiences are not accompanied by increased empathy, kindness and wisdom, their spiritual value is questionable, to say the least. Just because a message or experience emanates from 'supernatural source' does not mean it needs to be obeyed.

"It takes," as they say, "two to Tango." So there is always the interaction of an objective experience, the mental lens through which we perceive the object, and the subjective interpretation of the experience. It is up to us to determine the validity and meaning of any experience.

"THE NATURALIST"
THE WAY OF NATURE

*The Naturalist is most at ease when surrounded by nature,
whether in the forest, the desert, the plains, the mountains,
streams, lakes or the oceans of the natural environment,
in harmony with all the shared elements of existence.*

Is your connection with nature sacred?

Is nature your church or place of worship?

Do you feel a special affinity with animals or plants?

Do you feel tranquility, oneness or an inter-being-ness
when immersed in the natural world?

IT IS STRANGE AND TRAGIC that so many people have come to see
themselves as separate from nature. And even when they admit
that they are a part of nature, many still insist that human beings
are at the top of the evolutionary ladder, a superior species, chosen
by God (or Darwin) to be in charge of all the other minerals, plants,
and animals of the Earth. This bias toward human superiority
can be found in many of the world's religious, philosophical and
scientific traditions. Fortunately, within these same traditions,
there are other voices that lead us back into sacred communion
with nature—the mother of us all.

Sadly, our separation from the natural world has led us to
become obsessively fixated on human relationships and the things
we do and make. Having forgotten our symbiotic, interdependent
place in the natural world, we desperately look for happiness and
satisfaction in the things that we manufacture from the world's
natural resources. We have been so clever with our intellects,
and our five-fingered hands, and yet, we have made ourselves so
terribly unhappy and dissatisfied with them!

It is also clear that this attitude to nature is not serving the long-term survival of ourselves or other species. Global climate change, species loss and massive environmental degradation are the consequence of human ignorance and arrogance. But perhaps it is beginning to dawn on even the most intransigent among us that human health and happiness ultimately depend on the health and balance of the natural environment as well.

Faced with impending environmental collapse, human beings are slowly admitting that we have neither the wisdom nor the tools to control and govern the Earth's natural systems based on our current and faulty premises for happiness. We are finally coming to the realization that our very existence is interdependently entwined with the elements and forces of nature.

Fortunately, it is still possible to restore our personal connection with the rest of nature. And, as we do so, we can also restore balance to our lives, replenish the health of nature and live sustainably with the environment. We can re-learn how to find peace and happiness through our relationship with the natural world. We can replace our obsession with the dissatisfying (though convenient) life-style that has so damaged the Earth with a new, joyful satisfaction based on living in harmony with nature.

Toward this end, it helps to remember that our physical bodies are composed of the same elements as the other living beings on earth. We are composed of trillions of living cells, most of which are *not human*. We are actually mobile eco-systems, overflowing with organisms that consider our bodies their home. Our skin is actually a semi-permeable membrane through which micro-organisms constantly flow. Our in-breath is filled with the oxygen produced by the Earth's flora, and our out-breath with the carbon dioxide that the plants need for their own survival.

Reconnecting with nature happens so easily when we sit quietly in nature and allow our minds to cease their incessant activity— when we allow ourselves to breath in and out, gently and naturally, and let go of our false sense of superiority and separation. It is only then that we can begin to intuit directly and embody our interconnectedness, our interdependence, our reciprocity and our interbeing with nature.

Sitting by a stream, we integrate ourselves into the flow of its waters. We comingle with the plants that are the source of our life-giving breath. We dance in the wind with butterflies who have recently been transformed from caterpillars. We sing with the birds, howl with the wolves, warm ourselves by a campfire whose heat we also produce in our own bellies. When we allow ourselves to rest in the mystery of our shared existence, we begin to touch the essence of our shared being—the creative force that is beyond our ability to conceive or to name. In this joining, we are of one spirit.

This is our original state of being. And when we are able to reconnect with it, we are refreshed, enlivened, inspired and rejuvenated. We begin living our lives in harmony with the natural world, without damaging the precious diversity of life and disrupting nature's finely tuned eco-systems. From that moment on, we cannot see ourselves as morally and intellectually superior, and we realize that we are not entitled to ruthlessly use nature for our selfish, short-term purposes. We begin to temper our actions with the wisdom of our interdependence and fulfill our responsibility to care for the natural world from which our own life has sprung. This, then, might be called the Way of Nature.

THE WAY OF NATURE IN BUDDHISM AND MY OWN LIFE

In the late 1990s, one of my Tibetan Buddhist teachers, Khensur Lobsang Donyo, came for a visit to my home near Aspen, Colorado, and gave teachings on meditation. During that week, we had a series of classes in town, and then on Sunday, we all drove out to a beautiful location nestled in an Aspen grove surrounded by the mountains. We were perched above a valley where our eyes could follow a pure mountain stream that meandered down from a high alpine lake beneath Capital Peak. This valley was a kind of altar for my personal relationship with nature. It is in this stream that I have asked my children to sprinkle my ashes when I die.

That morning, looking over this valley, Khensur spoke in Tibetan and I translated into English. He gave instructions on how to cultivate a meditation called *shamatha* that can produce mental equanimity, bliss, mindful-focus, and extraordinary states of consciousness. Then, each of our participants wandered off to meditate amidst the beauty of that place, while Khensur and I sat near each other engaged in our respective meditations.

After about an hour, everyone returned for a discussion on their experiences with this meditation and to hear Khensur's advice on how to continue their practice. The group was very grateful for this special opportunity and inspired to persevere in the practice. Then we all walked down the trail to the place where our vehicles were parked and began the drive back to town. I asked Khensur how he felt about the teaching and the surroundings. His answer took me by surprise.

He said, "I enjoyed my time with these students. Their questions were good, and they all seem motivated to cultivate a meditation practice. But . . . why did we have to come all the way out here?"

My immediate response was, "Because it is such a beautiful, peaceful, inspiring place to meditate." To that, Khensur just chuckled and said no more.

This exchange made me question my own assumptions about my own meditative practice, and whether I was inappropriately depending on 'nature' to be the cause of a pleasurable meditative experience. After all, I had experienced both blissful and horrific aspects of nature and had seen how my own states of mind changed in the midst of a storm that threatened my life. Khensur's loving chuckle made me aware that I might be depending on nature to be the cause of my own experiences. I began to re-examine the Buddhist admonition against reliance on an external cause for personal enlightenment and liberation. Relying on material objects, sensory stimulation or even nature are doomed strategies. The Buddhist Way of Nature begins within the mind of each person, for it is through this mind that we relate to all things, including nature. Therefore, sustainable happiness and equanimity in nature must begin within each of us. In my experience, this is the Buddhist nuance to the Way of Nature.

Generally, when it comes to religious and spiritual practice, there is a tendency to seek refuge or unification with a sacred reality that is external to our own mind. This sacred reality is often imbued with such divine characteristics as love, wisdom, omniscience, protection and healing. It is often felt to be a permanent, unchanging source that is omnipresent and available to us when we are in deep prayer, meditation or spiritual communion. If our natural spiritual path is one of nature, we might find that we meld into a state of being that transcends our normal ways of conceptualizing and perceiving the world. We are relieved of the stress that accompanies our careers and relationships. Our finite self dissolves into an infinite reality that feels as if it is in tune with the source of all existence. If, or when this happens, one might cling to the notion that our experience in nature is caused by a sacred or divine presence that is external and separate from the subjective mental elements we are bringing to the experience.

From a Buddhist perspective, every experience, including the one I just described, emerges because of the confluence of the external objects of perception and our internal presuppositions, our conditioned assumptions and our ways of knowing. So, even our sublime experiences in nature are also a reflection and projection of the internal baggage or wisdom we bring with us into the world of nature. Even in nature, there is a radical interdependence between the perceived and the perceiver.

So, the Buddhist Way of Nature also factors in our human nature and the causal interaction between our own states of mind and the states of being we encounter in nature. This helps us to fully experience the interdependence of being and prevents us from becoming attached to the appearances of nature as the independent cause of our happiness and well-being. For, in truth, nature is always changing. At times, it is friendly and supportive of our vulnerable human bodies. At other times, it threatens our physical existence. Therefore, the objects we perceive in nature, and the qualities we ascribe to them, are interdependently enmeshed with each other and with our perception of them. Both the external and internal causes of perception, as well as the experiences they engender, are empty of independent, inherent reality. It is this insight that deepens the Way of Nature and amplifies the experience of interdependence with all that exists.

The question for all of us is this—How can we alter our behavior towards the natural environment? It is quite clear by now, that our left-brain, scientific approach to nature is not sufficient by itself to stop our over-consumption of energy, our carbon emissions and destruction of eco-systems. Perhaps the missing ingredient is the loss of our primitive, intuitive sense of the sacred in nature. For example, if we believe in a divine creator or creative force that we call God, Allah, Brahman, or Wakantanka, we can intentionally recondition our minds to see that all of the plants, animals and minerals are an integral part of the Creator's divine state of being. We can see that by wantonly harming them, we are damaging the divine force that gave us life, and the foundation of the life for everything we know. From a spiritual perspective, we can re-unite our sense of the sacred with our intellectual understanding and energize all the other archetypal spiritual styles within us to change our behavior and preserve the miracle of life forever.

"THE PRAYER"
THE WAY OF PRAYER

The Prayer naturally seeks wisdom,
guidance, help, strength, healing or forgiveness from a
sacred being or divine source whose capabilities
supersede those of ordinary human beings.

Do you receive a special peace and tranquility when you pray?

Do you feel that prayer is an essential part of spiritual practice?

Do you have a daily prayer for help, guidance or protection from a higher power?

Do you believe that there are transcendent beings that can hear your prayers and help you?

WHY DO WE PRAY? Many of us turn to prayer when we need help with a problem so grave, a situation so complex, an emergency so dire, a relationship so painful, an illness so severe, a pain so excruciating, that we simply cannot solve it ourselves and there is no where else to turn.

Prayer activates an aspect of our consciousness that is different than our normal desires, wishes or hopes, for it engages the whole of our being. We put our whole selves into prayer—all of our energy, and our total focus. We mobilize a force within us that has the capacity to communicate with the transcendent dimension.

Our prayers might come in the form of songs, poetry, chanting or even dance. They might be accompanied by music, incense, ritual, or tears. They might be transmitted simply in silence, through focus on our breath, or meditation on a sacred symbol, word or truth. But, for many us, the rote prayers we once memorized, and the tidy beliefs that we were taught as children, no longer hold meaning for us or give us solace. We are haunted by questions that are still unanswered. We doubt the existence of the higher power to whom our parents and clergy taught us to pray; and we are left with the question: When I truly need to pray, to whom, or to what should I pray? We find that we are simply unable to pray fully until we redefine or re-imagine that higher power, that divine being, or that sacred essence with whom we seek to connect.

Since prayer requires a wholehearted engagement, our effort is sometimes stymied because one part of us is praying while another is in doubt. Therefore, in order to fully engage in prayer, we are forced to resolve our doubts by finding answers to such questions as: *Is there a higher power, or are there spirit beings who can hear my prayer and help me? Is there a higher state of consciousness within that can help me rise to this occasion? Can sincere and honest prayer in some way influence the forces of nature to come to my rescue?*

Furthermore, if prayer requires us to bring our whole being into the act of praying, we must find ways to bring our own natural spiritual styles, or ways of being, into the process. By recognizing and honoring our own unique predispositions for spiritual practice, we forge a way of praying that aligns with these. In this way, we utilize the arts, our body, our contemplation and meditation, our devotion, our imagination, our love and compassion, our mystical capacity, our interbeing with nature, our reason, our relationships and our wisdom. In other words, we activate our unique set of spiritual styles in the service of the Way of Prayer. Simply put, we learn to bring the totality of our authentic self into our prayers. In this way, the Spiritual Paths Mandala provides a context and a process for us to bring the whole of our being into the simple act of praying.

THE WAY OF PRAYER IN BUDDHISM AND MY OWN LIFE

On the day before my thirty-fourth birthday, I was riding my motorcycle toward the Kulu Valley in north-western India. I had departed earlier that day from the annual conference of Fulbright Scholars at a grand old hotel in the town of Simla, the former summer capital of the British Raj. I was in India to complete my doctoral research on the *Perfection of Wisdom Sutra* and used my motorcycle to take me on adventures throughout northern and southern India. I was also traveling with a 16mm movie camera that I used to shoot scenes for the documentary film I was then making on Buddhism. On the back of the motorcycle was a specially built box to store the camera, a sound recorder, tripod and extra film. The weight of this gear made the motorcycle a bit unbalanced and I had to take care, especially when parking it and putting it on its kickstand.

Ever since I was a boy, I harbored a fear of dying during my thirty-third year, and this weighed on my mind as the cycle wound around the narrow mountain roads toward a government guesthouse perched high above the valley where I would spend the night. Near the end of the day, about ten miles from my destination, I rounded a bend in the road, and the valley opened up before me bathed in the cross light of the setting sun. It was so gorgeous that I stopped, perched the motorcycle on its stand, removed my motion picture camera from its case and filmed the scene laid out before me. I was truly enraptured by the scene and filled with awe and gratitude.

When I was done filming, I put the camera and equipment back on the motorcycle. Just then, it became unbalanced and began to fall. Instinctively, I grabbed hold of the first thing I could grasp, which turned out to be the exhaust pipe! It was still searingly hot and I burned my hand badly. I saved the motorcycle from tumbling over the cliff, but my right hand was terribly burned and huge blisters quickly covered my entire palm. With my left hand, I opened my first aid kit, grabbed a tube of antiseptic cream and slathered it over my right hand. Now, my challenge was to operate the motorcycle with just my left hand and the tips of the fingers of my right hand. It was a painful and tenuous ride back to the guesthouse.

As I rode, the old premonition of my death ran through my mind. I had just about six hours remaining in my thirty-third year, so I began to pray to the spirit of the Buddha and any other beneficent powers who could hear me: "Please help me to live through my thirty-third year and I will devote my life to doing good in the world!" As the guesthouse came into view, I was truly grateful to be alive. But when the innkeeper saw my right hand, he was horrified. It was obvious that I needed medical attention, but there was none to be found in this remote region of India.

That night, I sat before the fire in my room and continued with my prayers and meditations. I was determined to see if prayer and meditation could help heal my hand. When I had finished, I slept soundly through the night, only waking up when the innkeeper brought me my morning tea. Together, we looked at my right hand, and to our amazement, saw that it was completely healed! There was barely a sign of the severe burn. I was thus able to continue my journey and I have never forgotten my prayerful promise, nor the power of prayer and meditation.

During my years of Buddhist study, I have discovered the central importance of prayer in a fully developed practice. Buddhists are devoted the Buddha as a doctor, the Buddhist community as the nurses, and to the Buddha's teachings as the medicine. Buddhists pray to the unseen spiritual presence of the Buddha and the Bodhisattvas for help, guidance, wisdom and healing. They pray for the welfare of their families, communities and all beings. They pray to achieve personal liberation and enlightenment so that they can help others.

The Buddhist Way of Prayer is a very practical and powerful means of focusing our entire mind. It activates our own inner capacity to actualize those qualities and values for which we fervently long. But it also requires us to take personal responsibility for our actions and intentions, and to wholeheartedly engage in the purposes for which we pray. Buddhist prayer, it seems to me, does not solely rely on the divine intervention of an external being to do it all for us. So it is up to each of us to either create our own prayers or to infuse the prayers that we have been taught with a deeper sense of meaning and purpose. Otherwise, a prayer might just become a rote exercise that lacks the energy, intention and the commitment required to transform our prayer into a reality.

"THE THINKER"
THE WAY OF REASON

*The Thinker needs to figure things out
and create a reasonable foundation for
all aspects of spiritual practice.*

Do you need a good reason before beginning a spiritual endeavor?

Do you like to ponder the universal questions of existence?

Do you regard reason as a foundation for a spiritual practice?

Do you naturally ask the big 'why?' questions, rather than the more mechanical 'how?' questions?

WE ALL HAVE FRIENDS who love to ponder such issues as the nature of human existence, the origin of the universe, the purpose of life, the possibilities of life after death, the reasons for human suffering and the existence of God. Whether they know it or not, these people may be natural born metaphysicians whose spiritual archetype compels them to seek universal truths that lie beyond the reach of direct empirical observation and scientific study. Often, such people find it difficult to engage in prayer, ritual, devotion or meditation without a well-thought-out reason for doing so. But once convinced through reason, their practice can be unshakable. The dark side of the way of reason is incurable skepticism and negative judgments about those who engage in a spiritual practice without a solid intellectual foundation.

Albert Einstein, one of the greatest thinkers of all time, said, "Science without religion is lame, and religion without science is blind." He also spoke of a "cosmic religious feeling" that inspired him to discover the laws of God that govern the universe. He said, "I am of the opinion that all finer speculations in the realm of science spring from a deep religious feeling." Regarding this feeling, he wrote, "In my view, it is the most important function of art and science to awaken this feeling and keep it alive in those who are receptive to it." God, he said, "can be conceived only through the rationality or intelligibility of the world which lies behind all scientific work of a higher order."** Perhaps his most famous quote is, "God does not play dice with the universe."

More recently, the Dalai Lama has proposed that there is a shared underlying purpose for both scientists and spiritual practitioners. Both yearn to discover the deepest truths of existence. Indeed, the Dalai Lama's own Gelugpa school of Tibetan Buddhism provides a twenty-year long curriculum that blends rigorous intellectual study with serious spiritual practice. Their method has remarkable similarities to other spiritually inspired intellectual traditions, like the Habad Hasidic tradition of Judaism and the Jesuit Order of Catholic Christianity. The Way of the Reason was exemplified in the ancient academy of Plato who saw logical inquiry as a means to eternal wisdom, goodness and happiness.

A seeker on the Way of Reason strives to use logical inference and empirical observation as the basis for determining realities that lie beyond our cognitive and sensory perception. It seeks certainty about a reality that transcends our transient world, that is the foundation for being, that connects all phenomena and gives meaning and purpose to our lives. The Way of Reason seeks to prove, for example, the existence of an immortal soul, life after death, the existence or non-existence of God. It seeks a rational basis for meditation, prayer, devotion, ritual, mystical intuition and social service. The Way of Reason seeks a rational foundation for spiritual practice, believing that, if one has good reasons to back up one's spirituality and ethics, then it will be easier to pursue a spiritual life with rigor and consistency. But it is not uncommon for the Thinker to have a satisfying, rational description about the nature of reality, and yet, lack a healthy and satisfying spiritual life. For, often, they have not cultivated other qualities necessary to propel them along the way, like the aspiring mountain climber, with the proper theory and technique, but without the endurance and the other tools necessary to climb.

Sadly, a strictly intellectual perspective, isolated from other

---

* Well-known quotes made by Einstein at various times.

spiritual styles, like the Ways of Love and the Body, leads to its own form of psychological dysfunction and prevents the development of a satisfying personal spiritual path and a balanced life. So, the first step for the Thinker is to seek out and define the physical activities, the art forms, the prayers, the meditations and relationships, etc., that will conform with their intellectually defined higher truth, and then consciously integrate these into a practice.

The Way of Reason can also support other spiritual styles. For example, if our primary style is Love or Devotion, we might occasionally need a few good reasons to help us persevere through those inevitable times when spiritual practice loses its meaning and purpose. Similarly, if we only utilize the archetypal style of intellect, then our path will become awfully dry, lacking the invigorating energy that comes from contrast. Therefore, it is 'reasonable' for highly intellectual people to expand their repertoire of styles to enrich and enliven their personal spiritual path!

THE WAY OF REASON IN BUDDHISM AND MY OWN LIFE

In April of 1978, I arrived at Sera Monastery to work intensively on the *Perfection of Wisdom Sutra* with Geshe Lobsang Tenzin, who was then regarded as one of the most esteemed teachers in the monastery. I carried with me a letter of introduction from my Ph.D. advisor and spiritual teacher, Geshe Lhundup Sopa, who was also regarded by many Sera monks to be their senior teacher. And seeing as we all had the same teacher, I was easily welcomed into the monastery as a kind of spiritual brother.

I had arrived there with some trepidation, realizing that I would be the only non-Tibetan in the monastery and there would be no other English speakers. And though I had learned to read Tibetan, my ability to speak it still left a lot to be desired. My goal was to study the ancient texts of Tibet and India with a classically trained teacher who could provide me with the all-important oral commentary essential for understanding the written scriptures. This work was all-the-more poignant for me because I knew the monks at Sera were refugees from the repressive Chinese occupation of Tibet. They had come to India in order to preserve the ancient teachings of Buddhism that were being wiped-out in their homeland.

The sun was just beginning to set when I arrived, and I began meeting all the monks in the small compound in which I would study. As we sat on a small porch sipping tea, I began hearing what sounded like a riot of shouting and loud claps of hands several hundred yards away. This was the last sound I expected to hear in a Buddhist monastery! "What is all that noise?" I asked. To which they replied, "That is the sound of the afternoon debate." Interested, I walked up the path, accompanied by a couple of others, to see hundreds of red-robed monks spread out on the great lawn in front of the temple enthusiastically debating the meanings of the scriptures they had been studying. They were carrying on a tradition of learning that began in India more than two thousand years ago!

In the debate, two rows of monks sit facing each other. At the center of one end stands the monk who swirls in a dance-like motion and loudly claps his hands as he fires questions at another monk who is seated before him at the center of the opposite end the two rows. Often, the debate becomes marvelously animated, as other monks jump to their feet to deliver the argument. In this way, intellectual activity engages their bodies as well as their minds. The debate becomes a physical expression and release that is especially important for teenage monks engaged in rigorous study.

This system of education at Sera Monastery follows the philosophy of the Gelugpa school of Tibetan Buddhism that was inherited from ancient India's Nalanda Monastery. This approach includes three primary stages: (1) Learning; (2) Contemplating; and (3) Meditating. The Learning component includes reading, memorizing, debating with fellow students, and studying with a teacher. Here, students learn the whole of Buddhist philosophy, epistemology, logic, ethics, ritual, prayer and metaphysics. The curriculum can also include art, medicine and astrology. Along with the Stage of Learning, students also engage the Stage of Contemplation or deep reflection on the meaning of that which is being learned. Finally, students practice the Stage of Meditation in order to develop profound and direct insight into the truths they have learned and contemplated.

This approach to Buddhist study and practice appealed to me at that point in my life because my own archetypal spiritual style, the Way of Reason, naturally sought rational explanations to support my own evolving spiritual practice. For example, I found that meditation, devotion and ritual without the support of reason did not quell my questions and doubts. I felt that meditative quiescence alone was not a sufficient foundation for my transformation, and that I needed to engage my other learning styles on this journey. I needed to activate and satisfy my other ways of knowing, and to bring into alignment the various archetypal personality types that were competing for primacy in my unconscious mind.

The educational system at Sera Monastery was developed in ancient India, which like ancient Greece, had great centers of spiritual, intellectual and mystical learning. In the fifth century B.C.E., Buddhism emerged from a vibrant religious and philosophical culture that engaged the mind, body and spirit holistically. The Indian intellectual traditions provided logical reasons to strengthen and support spiritual practice, thereby helping serious practitioners to progress on their paths to enlightenment unencumbered by doubt and skepticism.

The Buddhist Way of Reason covers nearly every facet of the Buddha's teachings, as well as the various interpretations of these teachings. It helps the mind to explore all the possible permutations and consequences of difficult doctrines. It helps the practitioner to gain clarity and to refine the objects of meditation. In the case of emptiness, the Buddhist ultimate truth, the Way of Reason helps to define and contextualize this enigmatic proposition and leads the mind into a specific form of insight meditation *(vipashyana)* in which Emptiness can be directly and non-dually perceived by the meditator. By first understanding the non-paradoxical logic of emptiness, the meditator can eventually hold the meditative insight on emptiness without falling into the extreme of nihilism. After years of practice, they can simultaneously perceive both the ultimate and conventional nature of existence. This enables them to engage compassionately in the world, while at the same time being liberated from the causes of their own suffering.

For the Gelugpa and other similar schools of Buddhist education, the Way of Reason is a necessary prerequisite for the imaginal and mystical practices of the Buddhist Tantras. Yet the intellectual path alone is not a sufficient condition for enlightenment and liberation and must be integrated with and supported by the other ways of learning and knowing.

Through my later work with spiritually mature colleagues of different spiritual traditions, I have found that their paths encompass all the twelve archetypal spiritual styles. As they developed along their respective paths, they have discovered and immersed themselves in the rich intellectual traditions that reside within their chosen religion. They exemplify how the intellect can be a handmaiden in the spiritual journey.

"THE MENSCH"
THE WAY OF RELATIONSHIPS

*The Mensch learns most naturally and expresses
spirituality through compassionate interaction with
others, gaining deep satisfaction thereby.*

Do you gain wisdom primarily through relationship
with others?

Do you prefer the company of others to solitude?

Do you like to help others to learn, solve problems and
become happy?

Do you enjoy being involved in community projects for
the common good?

FROM THE MOMENT of our conception until we take our final
breath, we are constantly in relationship with others. It is
through relationships that we learn to apply that which we have
learned. For some of us, relationships are the primary vehicle
for learning, while others may prefer a more solitary absorption
in the intellect or meditation. Every profession and relationship
provides equal opportunity for manifesting our inner values
and insights. Whether one is a lawyer, a soldier, a minister, a
politician, a health care professional or a businessperson, one can
be in relationship with others in ways that can meet our highest
ethical standards.

Relationships are our constant joy and challenge. Through
relationships, we see reflections of ourselves and experience
our shared human condition, as reflected in the lives of
others. Relationships are the stage and playground for
love and hatred, compassion and narcissism, wisdom and
ignorance. Relationships are the basis for a life-long ethical
experiment—the living laboratory for testing *if* and *how* generosity

actually generates personal happiness, and *if* and *how* selfishness generates sadness.

It is through relationships that we are able to learn how virtuous and non-virtuous intentions can affect our relative states of happiness and well-being. By experiencing joy, grief, love and jealousy—and by the dispassionate observation of these emotions—we recognize the intentions that produce lasting happiness, and those that produce sorrow.

Through relationships, we observe the effects of religious and spiritual teachings on others. We experience directly the personal effects of spiritual teachings as we try to apply them in our interactions with others. The Way of Relationships might also include our direct interaction with ideas and intentions, and with the spiritual deities that are their manifestation. Many great spiritual traditions report of how spiritual fulfillment results from an intimate relationship with a deity, a holy spirit, an ancestor or divine principal.

The Way of Relationships might also be called the Way of Service, for it is through relationship that we serve the deepest needs of others. It is in relationship that we experience sympathy for others—the deep recognition of shared suffering and empathy—a profound connection with the soul, spirit or essence of another being. Sympathy and empathy are the fuel for our journeys along the spiritual Way of Relationships.

It is through relationships that we actualize the other spiritual propensities within us. One of many powerful examples of the spiritual Way of Relationships is that of a healer. Healing is compassionate spirituality-in-action, for it aims to alleviate both symptoms and the many interconnected causes of suffering. Therefore, healing the source of the illness might be regarded as a more profound intention than that of the Hippocratic Oath to "do no harm."

Our ability to heal others is proportional to our own personal depth of empathy, wisdom, and our spiritual realization. Conversely, our own spiritual realization and fulfillment depends on the sincerity of our compassionate intention to heal others. If our spiritual intention is limited by self-centeredness or narcissism, we will be unable to achieve our own spiritual freedom; for narcissism is the antithesis of empathy and interdependent reciprocity. Self-absorption only increases our isolation and misery.

Healing, of course, does not merely focus on the physical health of human beings. For true healing is holistic and takes into consideration the totality of all the interdependent elements that must be aligned to create a healthy being. Therefore, a spiritual approach to healing doesn't merely focus on the physical; its scope includes the interdependent psychological, nutritional, emotional, and environmental (including the subtle spiritual anatomy of our physical existence). An InterSpiritual approach to health recognizes the shared wisdom teachings on healing from all the world's great spiritual traditions.

Because the field of healing is vast and complex, becoming a healer must focus on a form of healing that is most compatible with our own life-experience, life-goals and our other archetypal spiritual styles. Depending on our personal abilities, we might specialize in any number of disciplines, including: Psychology, Ministry, Philosophy, Conflict Resolution, Medicine, Chiropractics, Osteopathy, Massage, Yoga, Chi Gong, Environmental Health, Public Health, Ecological Restoration, Permaculture, Renewable Energy, and Public Policy.

As healers, we can choose to heal people's physical illnesses, psychological wounds, anger and hatred, and even broken relationships between friends, partners, families, ethnic groups, racial groups, religious groups, tribes and nations. But one doesn't need a professional credential to be a healer. Each moment of our lives we are in relationship with others—with people, animals, plants and our physical environment. Therefore, every moment provides us with an opportunity for kindness. If our career is compassion, life itself is an equal opportunity employer.

As spiritual healers, the foundation for our practice is our compassionate intention. Our compassion moves us to alleviate the symptoms and ultimate causes suffering, and to help both ourselves and others find true and lasting happiness. As spiritual healers, we are not required to satisfy immediate whims and desires. Rather, through our acquired wisdom, we can help people to develop the long-term causes of eternal happiness and eliminate the long-term causes of perpetual suffering. And as we do, we might contemplate the words of Jesus, quoted in Luke 4:23, "Physician, heal thyself."

Although I have focused on healing in talking about the Way of Relationships, I tend to think of the person who follows the Way of Relationships as a Mensch—a Yiddish word for a 'human being,' but having the connotation of being a superior person—someone who simply wants to do good in the world by interacting positively with other people in such a way as to benefit others. The Mensch thinks, "I am happiest when I am doing good for others." But, as many of us know, the desire to do good is not always sufficient for accomplishing it. And, it might even make us vulnerable to others who would take advantage of our giving nature. When this happens, we sometimes shut down our instinctive desire to help others. Sometimes we become cynical, or close ourselves off from others.

Therefore, the Mensch can benefit from a rational intellectual examination about what is *truly good* for others, rather than simply satisfying their immediate wants and desires. The Way of Reason might help the Mensch to discern the best method to help a person get what they need rather than just what they want. The wisdom of Plato, the Buddha, King Solomon, Jesus, Muhammad, Martin Luther King Jr. and Lao Tzu might be good resources, helping us discern what is in people's long-term interests.

If your spiritual style is the Way of Relationships, then you can form the core of your spiritual learning and practice around your desire to serve others. In the Hindu traditions, this path is called "Karma Yoga," the spiritual path of service. Yet, in order to fully actualize our desire to serve others, Hindu sages advise us to cultivate the paths of wisdom (Jnana Yoga), meditation (Raja Yoga), and devotion (Bhakti Yoga). When we have brought all these archetypal styles into harmony, then we are able to heal ourselves as we help others heal themselves.

THE WAY OF RELATIONSHIPS IN BUDDHISM

When I first began my Buddhist practice over four decades ago, I was attracted to the Buddhist notion of non-attachment. It was a healthy, athletic, fun time in my life, so the dour Buddhist "Truth of Suffering" seemed a dramatic overstatement. It seemed to me that my occasional unhappiness and dissatisfaction simply came from my attachment to people and things. When relationships turned sour, I was unhappy. So I concluded that if I just stopped being attached, I would be happier. In other words, I tried to avoid committed relationships!

Later, I learned that this wasn't at all what the Buddha had in mind when he taught non-attachment. He wasn't advising us to avoid relationships and engagement in the world. Rather, he was imploring us to be compassionately and lovingly engaged, while at the same time, not being attached to a false expectation that people and things had the power to make us happy. The Buddhist goal, I learned, is not to withdraw and disengage from relationships, but to wisely and compassionately engage with others to make the world a better place.

It seemed ironic that the Buddha taught an inner, solitary path of meditation, while at the same time, requiring practitioners to cultivate compassionate relationships with others. Yet, I learned that Buddhist practice is at once solitary and relational. It recognizes the interdependence that exists between our inner states of mind and our perceptions of the external world. It recognizes that the quality of our relationships depends on the quality of our inner consciousness.

Buddhist practice is built on a foundation of love and compassion. Love *(metta)* is the sincere wish for the happiness of all beings, and compassion *(karuna)* is the intention to liberate all beings from the causes of suffering. Buddhism recognizes that our personal happiness and well-being are inextricably interconnected with our intention to help others. Yet Buddhism also recognizes that we cannot fully actualize our compassion and love without the internal wisdom that knows how to help. Wisdom requires meditation, and meditation requires training, discipline and long periods of silent, solitary practice. The theory is that our meditation practice will eventually help us engage in the world with wisdom and compassion.

The Way of Relationships in Buddhism often begins with one's relationship with a spiritual teacher or guide who has both deep knowledge and personal experience. It is up to each of us to find a teacher who can teach according to how we learn best. The Way of Relationships then leads us to be in relationship with our families, and in the community of others *(sangha)* with whom we can enjoy mutually supportive friendships. In community, with like-minded people, we can learn and discuss our personal challenges and rewards; we can meditate with each other and enjoy life-activities that are compatible with our highest ideals.

Finally, the Way of Relationships challenges us to enter

into compassionate, reciprocal relationships, with broader communities of friends and colleagues. Whether our professions or avocations are related to such fields as the environment, health care, business, professional services, public policy, education, public safety or raising a family, they all provide equal opportunities for wise, compassionate, ethical, 'right relationships' with others. For, it is in these relationships that we deepen our understanding of life, actualize our compassionate intentions, and evolve toward personal liberation and enlightenment.

"The Sage"
The Way of Wisdom

The Sage embodies the wisdom of a life
fully-lived and the truths transmitted by profound
wisdom-holders throughout the ages.

Do you long for the wisdom to guide your own life and help others?

Do you yearn for transcendent insight into the true nature of reality?

Do you aspire to the wisdom of the Buddha, Christ, Lao Tzu, Black Elk, Ramakrishna, Muhammad or Moses?

WISDOM IMPLIES a knowingness of truths harvested from the totality of one's life-experience. It surpasses the knowledge gained through mere intellectual conceptualization and empirical observation. It emerges from the synthesis of all our knowledge, gained throughout our lives, through the combination of physical, emotional and intellectual sources, infused and informed by perceptions that reach beyond ordinary appearances and mental projections of reality.

There is a deep reverence for Wisdom in many spiritual traditions, along with an implicit assumption that all humans are capable of achieving it. *Prajna* is the Mahayana Buddhist word for Wisdom. It connotes a direct perception of the Ultimate Truth—emptiness—which is an unmediated knowingness that is not filtered by concepts and the senses.

In Buddhism, as in some other traditions, Wisdom is associated with the Feminine, whereas the compassionate method for applying Wisdom is associated with the Masculine. *Sophia*, the Greek word for Wisdom, was adopted by Christianity to connote the knowledge of God that comes from a direct relationship with the divine. *Gnosis,* also a Greek word, has been used to connote a direct mystical insight and spiritual knowledge of the divine. *Hokhmah,* the Hebrew word for Wisdom, is also associated with the infinite knowledge of God and connotes direct intuitive insight into the essence or truth of existence. In Taoism, Wisdom is the quality of mind that is in harmony with the unnamable essence of the universe.

Within each of the world's great religions, there are esteemed individuals and small communities of contemplatives who are the holders of their Wisdom traditions. These Wisdom-holders have often studied or apprenticed with others who have been handed and themselves handed-down a lineal transmission from teacher to student, from one generation to the next. The sages in each generation have persevered in the ancient practices for gaining transcendental wisdom exemplified and taught by the founders and sages of their respective religions. The job of a Wisdom-holder is to reveal these truths in a contemporary idiom, to exemplify a way of life that is consistent with Wisdom, and to transmit the methods for gaining Wisdom to those who possess the requisite intention, capacity and fortitude.

THE WAY OF WISDOM IN BUDDHISM AND MY OWN LIFE

I remember clearly the day Geshe Sopa began to teach me about the Perfection of Wisdom. I was his graduate assistant, and we spent hours preparing his courses on Buddhism at the University of Wisconsin. In those days, there were hardly any books on Buddhism, and Buddhist Wisdom was still an enigma. I still remember how surprised I was by the process he described and how different it was from my preconceived notions.

Wisdom, he taught me, did not emerge solely from the accumulation of vast sums of knowledge. It did not arise solely from years of study, or even from the experiences of a long life, well-lived. Rather, Wisdom emerges when we have both accumulated profound knowledge and systematically eliminated all the obstacles that prevent our inner wisdom from arising. In other words, the practice of the Perfection of Wisdom entails both a positive *(cataphatic* or *via positiva)* and a negative *(apophatic* or *via negativa)* process that eradicates ignorance about the true nature of reality and purifies the negative emotions that cloud our capacity to clearly and directly perceive that which is real. This *via negativa* presupposes that we have the natural capacity to become wise once the obstacles have been removed. It assumes that knowledge filtered through concepts and sense perceptions is tainted by their inherent limitations.

One of the features of Buddhism that intrigued me most in the beginning was the proposition that all beings can become enlightened. All beings, according to Buddhism, have "Buddha Nature"—which is to say, the potential to become Buddhas. As human beings, we have a unique opportunity. We experience just enough suffering, and have just enough intelligence, to actually find our way out of the prison imposed by our ignorance.

The fundamental assumption here is that our minds have an innate capacity to be wise, and that this Wisdom emerges naturally when our mind is clear and unimpeded. Thus, Buddhism makes meditation a major focus of the spiritual path. According to its teachings, clarifying the mind is not unlike filtering the pollutants out of water. When our ocean-like consciousness is clouded by sub-surface currents of desire, and tossed about by the winds of sensory distractions, it cannot reveal the Wisdom that lies within its depths. But once these disturbing currents and winds have calmed down, the true nature of our existence is revealed and made clear.

Therefore, Buddhist meditations often begin with focused breathing to calm the winds of sensory distraction stirring the surface of our minds. One method is to begin by focusing on the breath as it enters the nostrils. Then, having established this preliminary focus, we allow our awareness to ride along the surface of our breath as it travels through the nasal cavities, down the throat, through the bronchial tubes and into the lungs. Our awareness then enters into the heart *chakra*, which resides near the center of the chest. This is the place that many traditions consider the center of our being, the abode of the soul, or the home of our core-consciousness. Breathing gently into the heart center, we let our awareness dwell there, peacefully. Breathing in this way, we gradually withdraw our awareness from the distractions of our five senses into our heart center where it can rest in undisturbed focus and equanimity.

Along with focused breathing, we also activate the capacity of our mind to watch for and observe any incoming thoughts or emotions that might disturb this silent focus on the breath. This is like the searchlight from an inner observation tower passively scanning the surface of the mind. When a potentially disturbing mental event is revealed, we simply take note of it and let it dissipate like a thin cloud in a blue sky. We might also observe how the distracting thought or emotion is impermanent, interdependent and empty of inherent existence.

Once the mind is calm, we can begin to pacify and empty-out the subconscious currents of desire and negative emotion caused by previous thoughts, actions and relationships. Just as we did with the surface winds of sensation, we now dissipate these disturbing inner currents by directing the wisdom of impermanence, interdependence, emptiness, love and forgiveness on them. By engaging in this meditation, the unconscious currents of *karma* and negative emotion are dissipated and our minds become clear and calm. In this way, we are able to purge the toxins of ignorance, distractions, and negative emotion swirling beneath the surface in our unconscious minds.

By observing the incessant thoughts and emotions churning beneath the surface of our minds while breathing mindfully, we can observe them dispassionately and objectively, clearing away the hidden residue of previous thoughts and actions that control our states of mind. We see that all of these external sensations and internal emotions arising and falling within us are impermanent, interdependent, and empty of inherent reality. See them as causal and therefore changeable. We realize that we can take control of them, rather than allowing them to control us.

By emptying our minds of ignorant projections, biases, and preconceptions, we are able to observe reality *as-it-is*, rather than how we are conditioned to see it. Rather than being emotionally swayed by the appearance of the things we see, hear, smell, taste or touch, we are immediately attuned to all the causal conditions that brought them into existence. We are not stuck on the appearance, but aware of all the factors that created them, and the effect these will have on the future. Once we are able to observe the world wisely, unimpeded by mental obstacles, our capacity to help others is infinitely expanded.

The Buddhist Way of Wisdom is not to have an encyclopedic knowledge of facts, names and dates. It is a Wisdom measured by *what we know* and *how we know*, resulting from a direct, intuitive perception about the nature of all things—one that is not confined to subject-object duality and projections conditioned by ignorance. The Buddhist Way of Wisdom recognizes the illusory appearances of normal perception and sees all the factors of their interdependence. It can intuit the past causes and future effects of any point in time. This Wisdom emerges when we have emptied our minds of the pollutants of ignorance, the undercurrents of *karma* and negative emotions, and the surface winds of sensory distraction.

The Buddhist Way of Wisdom, therefore, is a necessary condition for fulfilling ones compassionate vow to help others eliminate the causes of their suffering. In this way, the archetypal spiritual style of the Sage is balanced and actualized by the archetypal spiritual style of the Lover.

CONCLUSION

THE MAJOR RELIGIONS have all developed rituals, myths, metaphysics, aesthetics, meditations, prayers, etc., that match up to the natural archetypal styles residing in human beings everywhere. Implicitly, they have created tents and niches for everyone. However, as with all educational institutions, they often slip into a one-size-fits-all mode of education and practice.

Since each of us has all of these archetypal styles nascent within us, these need to be honored, utilized and brought into harmony. They provide us with a starting-point for spiritual practice, lead us toward our spiritual paths, and guide us through our most important journey.

Generally, we are unaware of the power these archetypal styles exert on our lives and the decisions we make. They provide the foundation for our choices, and yet, we hardly take notice of how they do this. But, once we have identified and honored these styles within us, we can begin to make conscious, intelligent choices about the formation of our spiritual paths.

One of the primary causes of spiritual dysfunction in today's world is that many of us have been unable to match our primary archetypal styles to the teachings and practices of a wisdom tradition. Therefore, we seek solutions in a myriad of non-traditional ways of thinking and practice and attempt to cobble together a path from a combination traditional and non-traditional practices. To help remedy this situation, the process illustrated by the Spiritual Paths Mandala helps us to engage in the development of our paths in a more systematic manner. We do so by utilizing our own primary spiritual archetypes to find the answers to our spiritual questions. We then integrate and balance all of our styles and apply our answers in the development of our path.

Once our spiritual foundation is secure, it supports, informs and gives purpose to one's whole life, no matter what one's profession or situation. It pervades all aspects and all moments of life—from nine to five at the office, to four to seven with the kids at home, and even Saturdays and Sundays in the company of family and friends. This foundation, or lack of it, affects everything we think, do and feel. So, without taking ourselves too seriously, the pursuit needs to be recognized as a serious one, worthy of our deepest and most abiding effort. Therefore, it is important to begin by identifying our own natural spiritual archetypal styles. As we progress down the path, it will be important to begin integrating other styles so that our understanding, action and experience form an integrated and solid foundation for our internal spiritual life and external engagement in the world.

PART II
THE TWELVE SPIRITUAL
QUESTIONS

INTRODUCTION

THERE COMES A TIME in our lives when we feel the urge to discover our true identities, the meaning and purpose beyond our normal activities, our relationships and our careers. This calling might arise from a personal crisis, the death of a loved one, a medical emergency or a relationship gone bad. This can be a scary time for many people; we sometimes find ourselves knocked out of the cogs of our very pattered lives, shaken from the directions that our parents and society laid out for us, questioning the decisions we have made about how we should live our lives.

While this can be a difficult time, it is also pregnant with possibility—for a new birth and a new lease on life. The tragedy for many of us, however, is that we don't take full advantage of these moments. We either sink into existential despair or seek distraction in sensuality, shopping, liquor, drugs, or other forms of entertainment. It is not that life's pleasures are evil; it's just that they distract us from life's central issues, such as discovering one's spiritual identity, purpose and meaning. Too often, the 'gift' of an existential crisis remains unopened because there is no one, no resource available to us to help us make the most of this grand opportunity.

The possibilities latent in uncertainty and loneliness are usually also left unexplored. We spend so much time and money distracting ourselves from the challenges and opportunities they bring. We build home entertainment systems to drown-out the silence of our inner sanctuaries. We run off to the movies, to parties, to bars, to events. We have our daily drinks and smokes, or head to the gym or exercise classes. We go shopping for things we want but do not need. We adorn ourselves with make-up, clothing and tattoos that make us look attractive or confident about our life-direction and choices. We do these things because we think they will make us happy. We do them to fend off the real questions of identity, meaning and purpose that await each of us in every moment of silence.

Two popular tactics for burying the 'big questions' is to arm ourselves with either skepticism or blind faith. The skeptic within us, with great confidence and certainty, often undermines the question before it is even asked, never allowing us to seriously engage or explore possible answers. On the other hand, some people simply ignore the big questions by clinging to blind faith in someone else's answers. They give their questions to 'professionals,' like priests, rabbis, and scientists and psychologists, then simply go along with the answers they give.

These strategies of distraction, skepticism, and blind faith, work for a good deal of our lives, but cracks in these defense mechanisms begin to appear when bad things happen to ourselves and those we love. They fail us in times of unavoidable silence and impenetrable boredom, and often fail to comfort us as we near the ends of our lives. It is in these inevitable moments of existential crisis that we must dig down deep within and reach for answers to the questions that have been with us since childhood. It is then that we must confront the questions that have been lurking in the shadows of our minds all our lives.

The solution, it seems to me, is to live our lives in full awareness of these questions, to accept them, and to embrace the adventures they present. I suppose this is easy for me to say, because questioning is natural to my archetypal style of being. Questions, for me, are the energizing juice of life. They have provided me with a life-long avocation, and have been the steady drum beat beneath the surface of my professional and personal life. I am enlivened by the search for answers, and thrilled by the marvelous variety of answers that come from both the lived-wisdom of ordinary people, and from the sages of the world's spiritual and scientific traditions. The answers I have deduced for myself have become pieces of a puzzle that I am gradually assembling to form a coherent spiritual path, and to undergird my active participation in the world.

Since all of us have questions, it is fortunate that there are so many resources for answering them. The adventure for us is to match up our primary learning style with a compatible teacher and tradition with whom we can explore and discover answers that guide our lives.

At the time of my own 'existential crisis,' the spiritual tradition that best matched my primary archetypal style was Buddhism.

But, over the years, I have explored other archetypal styles within me and have expanded my interest to other religions and spiritual traditions that have gradually helped to actualize and balance the different styles of my being.

My interest in Buddhism began with experimentation and a survey of various Buddhist traditions, including Zen and Theravada Buddhism, before finally settling on the Gelugpa school of Tibetan Buddhism, which is known for its emphasis on intellectual inquiry, in addition to meditation, ritual and Tantra. This tradition values scholarship and debate as a companion to contemplative practice, and provided me with a grounding for my primary archetypal styles, as well as a resource for answering my major spiritual questions.

Buddhism is an expansive and ancient tradition which has been dealing with universal questions for over 2,500 years. While there are some basic principles that underlie all Buddhist answers, there has always been a lively debate about the nuances and finer points. These debates begin with interpretations of the Buddha's teachings found in the scriptures. This approach to understanding the underlying principles of Buddhism provided a good starting point for me. Once grounded in a variety of opinions, I was free to decide for myself which was true. This approach has also guided my study of other religions and has helped me to refine personally satisfying answers that are not dictated by any single religious dogma.

In the following pages, I will explore many of our 'big questions' and sum up a few of the answers I have gleaned from my study and practice of Buddhism and assemble some the pieces of the puzzle. Due to limitations of space and time, I won't go into great detail about each of these questions. In exploring my personal answers, I am not speaking *for* Buddhism, but *from* my own experience with Buddhism and the wisdom I have gained from teachers of many different traditions. I am writing from my personal experience with Buddhism and the Buddhist answers that have personally resonated with me. That said, I have found that no religion has an exclusive claim on the truth. Each contributes nuances, refinements, and variations that enrich the human experience and the quest for universal wisdom.

In writing about *my own* answers, I am not trying to provide you with *the* answers. My intention is only to give you an example of how I have explored my questions in the hope that this will stimulate your own thinking and writing on each of the questions. By doing this, you will be able to assemble the puzzle pieces of your own personal spiritual path.

CONSCIOUSNESS

What is consciousness? What is its potential?
Is my consciousness confined to my brain and nervous system?
Is my personal conscious connected to a larger,
perhaps universal sphere of consciousness?

THE QUESTION OF CONSCIOUSNESS overlaps and encompasses all other questions and spiritual styles. But since the word 'consciousness' can be so all-encompassing, it is not easy to study, measure and describe. Some of its qualities are physical and relate to the body's sensations. Other qualities are mental and include thoughts, emotions, memories, desires, fears and hopes. Still other capabilities of consciousness might surpass our normal mental and physical senses and relate to intuition, clairvoyance, extrasensory perception, dreams and imagination.

Unlike the names of physical objects, the word 'consciousness' has no reference in the physical world. There is no fixed object that we can point to and call it 'consciousness.' Consciousness is the awareness that arises and follows from contact with the objects perceived by our eyes, ears, nose, tongue, skin and mind. So, to ask our selves 'What is consciousness?' is a bit like a mirror looking at a reflection of itself in another mirror and asking 'What is mirror?' Or, a thought asking itself 'What is thought?' It is the awareness being aware.

You see, consciousness is both the subject and the object of the question, 'What is consciousness?' For it is the foundation for everything we think, do, experience and say. And because the many functions of consciousness are the bases for our experience of life itself, the category of consciousness as a whole does not lend itself to a single, standard definition, quantification or valuation.

Our experience of consciousness is implicit in all our spiritual styles. For example, when we sail the ocean and gaze beyond the endless horizon, our body experiences conscious awareness of the wind and sun touching our skin. When we sit alone in the forest among the tall pines, our nose smells their sweet aroma and our ears hear the wind moan through the branches. When we stare into the rippling waters of a mountain stream, we feel it intermingling with our body and spirit. When we listen to the rapturous climax of Mahler's Third Symphony, our whole body pulsates with inner exhilaration. When we practice Yoga, we experience refined bodily awareness through our muscles, joints and energy centers. When we are in loving relationship with another person, we feel the bliss of our comingled existence. When we pray, we experience our healing energy going into someone who is ill. When we meditate, we experience awareness of awareness itself and at-one-ness with all of existence. When we dream, our experiences seem as real as when we are awake. When we lucidly observe and participate in the imaginal realm, we work with the images that condition our future states of being. When we are in deep sleep, we experience peaceful tranquility.

Our big questions all relate to the nature of consciousness:

Why am I here? Where did I come from? What is my life's purpose? What is real? What is my highest potential? How can I be transformed into my ideal being? What happens when I die?

Therefore, the answers to each of these questions also require us to grapple with the question of consciousness:

Is consciousness finite or infinite? Does it have a beginning and an end? Is it the product of my brain and nervous system? Does it survive the death of my body?

The Mandala Process provides an outline for exploring the vast subject of consciousness as it pertains to each of our spiritual styles, spiritual questions and spiritual practices.

MY OWN EXPERIENCE WITH THE QUESTION OF CONSCIOUSNESS

For Buddhism, transforming consciousness is the purpose of spiritual practice. For it is here that we can systematically evolve into enlightened beings to free others from suffering. Therefore, Buddhist psychologists and meditators have studied and named the myriad forms of consciousness as an empirical foundation for the art, science and practice of transformation.

Generally speaking, consciousness in Buddhism might be lightly summarized in the following ways: (1) sensory awareness that arises along with the sensations and perceptions of our ears, eyes, nose, tongue, and skin; (2) mental awareness that arises along with thoughts, concepts, memories and emotions, etc., that are in varying degrees associated with the physical brain and neurological system; (3) non-physical awareness, for example the states of consciousness that arise in deep states of meditation (that are not primarily dependent on the aforementioned physical sensory and mental activities).

All of these forms of awareness can contain a combination of both physical and non-physical properties in various degrees depending on the precipitating cause. The third type of awareness is primarily non-physical, therefore not solely precipitated by the brain and neurological system. In other words, this type of consciousness is capable of a transcendent awareness that is not dependent on or caused by physical sensations, thoughts, and emotions, etc.

Therefore, the Buddhist view of consciousness does not fit neatly with the materialistic view that consciousness is merely the function of the brain and neurological system. Nor does it mesh with theistic views that consciousness was created by God. The Buddhist view might also run counter to contemporary spiritual views that link consciousness with such metaphysical notions as primordial energy, the ground of being, or a universal consciousness that is the underlying cause for all that exists. From a Buddhist perspective, any metaphysical notion of a 'first cause' necessitates the next logical question: *What or who created the first cause of existence? If consciousness is the first cause, then how did it come into being?* For Buddhists, consciousness is simply an existential fact. While the Buddha didn't hypothesize its origin, he provided methods to harness its qualities for spiritual transformation.

The Buddha's approach to this age-old question about the origin of consciousness is formulated in his doctrine of dependent origination. Consciousness (i.e., awareness) exists as an integral element within a vast interdependent web of causes and effects. Conscious awareness, like everything else, is a constantly changing continuum without beginning or end. It is simply a necessary condition of all living beings in the infinite universe. Trying to find the 'first cause' of consciousness is an exercise in futility.

Yet this Buddhist answer does not seem to cure the human longing for a first cause of existence. Many non-Buddhists have looked to consciousness itself as a possible source of all existence, the ultimate ground of being. They have hoped Buddhism would support their notion of a primordial, universal consciousness that is the original cause of existence. In the past, I have been one of those people, so I understand the impulse. Unfortunately (or fortunately, as the case may be), classical Buddhism does not seem to satisfy this longing to make consciousness the first cause of existence.

However, there are some Buddhist schools of thought, for example, those influenced by Taoism in China and Vedanta in India, for which individual consciousness is thought to somehow meld into a universal Buddha consciousness at the time of enlightenment. There are also some Buddhist schools of thought that believe that the external world is simply a projection of our own consciousness. Similar theories of consciousness exist in many other religions and philosophies throughout the world. So again, the subject of consciousness, even within Buddhism, defies a simple answer!

NON-DUAL CONSCIOUSNESS

The term 'non-dual' consciousness is often used these days to describe a sacred state of awareness about the spiritual unity that exists between the individual soul and the divine source of all being. In this sense, we are 'all one,' and in unity with each other. We are interconnected in 'the oneness' of our being. Non-dual consciousness, therefore, is the awareness that we are all connected to, and created by, the same ultimate reality. We are 'one with' the ultimate source of our existence.

But as appealing as this notion of spirituality might be, it is not shared by classical Buddhism. Classical Buddhism looks at the term non-duality in several different ways. The nuances of these views are not easy to grasp. But understanding them is vitally important as a foundation for Buddhist meditation and the eliminating ignorance that is the cause of suffering. The following is my very brief synopsis of Buddhist views of non-duality drawn from the Buddhist philosophical tradition called *Prasangika Madhyamaka.*

(1) The first way of looking at non-duality requires an understanding of the Two Truths: the Conventional Truth and the Ultimate Truth. The Conventional Truth is that all phenomena are interdependent. A conventionally true phenomenon can be verified both empirically and logically by sense organs and minds that are unimpaired.

The Ultimate Truth is that all phenomena are empty of existing permanently, independently or inherently. Therefore, 'Emptiness' is the name given to the Buddhist Ultimate Truth. All phenomena, including our selves, embody both the Conventional and Ultimate Truth, i.e., we are all interdependent and empty. In that sense, all phenomena are non-dual. A non-dual consciousness simultaneously perceives these Two Truths about all phenomena.

(2) A second way of looking at non-dual consciousness is as follows. The objects that we perceive, and the qualities we ascribe to these objects, do not exist independently of our perception of them. For example, the perception that things are either inherently good or bad is subjectively imposed on objects of perception. These dualistic qualities don't exist inherently in the phenomena themselves. They are subjective projections, not objective realities.

Therefore, the things we perceive are 'empty' of these dualistic, paradoxical or contradictory characteristics. In our normal way of perceiving things, we tend to see things dualistically because we are socially conditioned and biologically wired to assume the qualities originate from the object itself. But, in fact, there is a radical interdependence between the object and the perceiver. Meditation on this interdependence and emptiness helps us to correct this misperception of reality and see things as they really are. This frees us from attachment to faulty appearances that cause desire, anger, greed, and other negative emotions that cause suffering.

(3) A third way is the meditative emptying-out of subject-object dualism. Here, the mind first rests in a tranquil state of equanimity and then focuses solely on the interdependence and emptiness of all phenomena, including our self. In those moments of meditative absorption, when the mind focuses directly on the emptiness of phenomena, there is no distinction of subject and

object—no distinction between the emptiness of the perceiver and the emptiness of that which is being perceived. Since the distinction of inner and outer emptiness does not appear in this moment of meditative absorption on emptiness, it is called 'non-dual consciousness.'

Therefore, the Buddhist views of non-duality do not connote a unity or oneness between the individual self and a universal creative force of all reality. Rather, Buddhist non-dual perception is a way of empirically, logically and meditatively seeing phenomena as they are, without projecting a grander metaphysical reality (like an uncreated Creator God) as the ultimate cause of their existence.

Varieties of Consciousness in Buddhism

In Buddhism, there are a variety of terms pertaining to the functions of consciousness. For example, the term 'feeling' *(vedana)* refers to the sensation (pleasant, unpleasant, or neutral) regarding an object that comes into contact with one of the five sense organs. Another is the term 'perception' *(samjna)* which occurs when the object is named and cognized. Then there are the various mental predispositions, thoughts, judgments, compulsions, opinions, etc. *(samskaras)* that arise once an object is perceived. Still another function is called 'conscious awareness' *(vijnana)* accompanies every sensory perception.

According to some Buddhist schools, there is also a type of consciousness called *yogi pratyaksha* that has the capacity to directly know or intuit reality without concepts and sense perceptions. This yogic consciousness emerges as the result of specific types of meditation. These Buddhist schools also identify a function called 'self-awareness' *(manas)* that is our awareness that we are aware, or the consciousness of our consciousness. This function of consciousness can lead to the illusion that there is a permanent subjective 'I' or 'self' that is the constant, unchanging perceiver behind every perception. From the Buddhist perspective, however, just because this function of consciousness encourages us to say things like, 'I think,' doesn't mean there actually is a permanent, independent 'I' behind every perception.

Finally, there is the function of consciousness that stores up all the karmic seeds of the past lives until they sprout as present and future perceptions, events and states of mind. This is called 'storehouse consciousness' or 'substrate consciousness' (alayavijnana).

These last two functions of consciousness can be misconstrued by those who long for proof of a permanent first cause of consciousness or 'ground of being.' This misunderstanding encourages people to assume that Buddhism implicitly believes there is a permanent self or consciousness that is the foundation for our existence. Based on this faulty assumption, they assert that the Buddhist notion of self and consciousness is the similar to the Hindu of Christian idea of the soul.

But the Buddhist view on a conscious self isn't so easily wrapped up into a neat little package. For consciousness itself is always changing in relation to the objects of which it is aware. And even though it appears to be the case, there is no permanent 'I' that remains unchanged as the subject of all experience. For the 'I,' like consciousness itself, is not separate from the interdependent chain of causation. Like everything else in the universe, it is impermanent, interdependent, and relational. The 'I' or 'self' is just a verbal convention for the subjective functions of consciousness. But it doesn't exist independently of the other elements of the body and mind.

According to some schools of Buddhism, direct yogic awareness of the illusory-empty nature of the 'I' and 'consciousness' is the transcendent perception that leads to ultimate liberation from suffering. It is through the direct realization of emptiness that we can become free to actualize our natural capacity for liberation, enlightenment, and spontaneous compassion.

The reassuring part of this Buddhist view is that consciousness is both interdependent and eternal. The challenging part of the Buddhist view is that consciousness is not the metaphysical foundation for existence. Therefore, it doesn't satisfy our longing for an unchanging, permanent foundation for being. From the Buddhist perspective, consciousness, like everything else, is interdependent. Like a river, consciousness is always flowing and changing from one life to the next in relation to the environment in which it runs. This view helps us to empty our minds of this notion of a permanent consciousness, soul or creator. And each time we empty ourselves of these notions, our mind opens more deeply into its natural wisdom. Cleansed of these misperceptions, we do not cling to objects and people as the source of our happiness.

Compassionately, we see people as they are, intuit the causes of their suffering and help them to be happy and free.

At the end of our physical lives, the non-physical functions of our consciousness, like yogic awareness, self-perception, and substrate consciousness, survive and migrate into a intermediate dreamlike state (*bardo*) of being before they incarnate again into physical form. From a Buddhist perspective, this is just a description of what happens with our consciousness, not a first-cause metaphysical explanation for 'why' it happens. The search for the first cause, according to Buddhism, is futile.

When we see our consciousness as separate, permanent and fixed, we constrict and limit our own infinite potential. But when we empty our minds of these self-limiting ideas and see ourselves as interdependent, relational, and infinitely expansive beings, we can then actualize our limitless potential for unbounded enlightenment. We can rest in a state of compassionate quiescence and interbeing with all of existence.

DEATH

What happens to my consciousness when my body dies?
Is death the end of me? How can death be an integral
part of my spiritual practice?

ISN'T IT REMARKABLE how our big questions can lay submerged beneath the excitement, distractions and mundane realities of daily life? They are the undercurrent of our conscious mind, only bubbling to the surface in times of tragedy, like the death of a close friend or relative. It is times like these that force us to confront the big questions in life.

This is especially true with the death of a young person, who is still capable of giving so much to the world. When this happens, we always ask: *Why did they die? Was it a random act in a chaotic universe? Was it ordained by God? Is there a reason?*

The death of friends and relatives reminds us that we don't really know what happens after we die. It focuses our attention on the crucial things that we must accomplish in our life. That is why we use the word 'deadline' for the time when a job must be completed. The deadline for the completion of our life's work will be the time of our own death. Since this could happen at any moment, we'd better get to our life's work now.

We all wonder what will happen to us when we die. The looming of the 'big unknown' moves us to seek answers in philosophy and religion; to ask the counsel of psychics and channels; to witness the trance-induced predictions of oracles; to sit in the presence of shamans who report experiences from other worlds; to find a spiritual tradition that can guide us from this life to the next.

In the Mandala Process, one gathers together views and conversations on death and immortality from many traditions and probes the answers to such questions as:

Is there a beginning or an end to me? What will become of me when I die?

MY OWN EXPERIENCE WITH THE QUESTION OF DEATH

Sitting up on an emergency room gurney, I struggled to get my wits about me. I had just died of a bee sting and been revived. The medic told me that I had no pulse and he didn't think he could bring me back. So I was grateful to be alive, but somehow, I still had a feeling of failure. For, after decades of Buddhist practice, I wasn't conscious through my dying. I had hoped to be fully present to the experience, and in a state of meditation that would have guided my consciousness toward my next incarnation into a being that could truly help this troubled world. But that's not how it was. I had a reaction to a bee-sting, and suddenly I collapsed, stopped breathing and was on my way out of this life.

On the morning after my death-by-bee-sting, I lay quietly and alone on my living room couch. I was in a bit of a daze, knowing that life would be different now, but I wasn't sure how. I had a strange sense that I had been graced with an opportunity to become a witness in the future unfolding of my own life's journey. This notion helped me to begin to shed many elements of my 'false self' that had been hanging on through my years of Buddhist practice, as well many restrictions and expectations for my life that had been imposed by society and family. Consciously, I became both the actor and the observer of my own life-story, and learned to "die before death," as my Sufi friends like to say.

Some years later, I got another chance to rehearse my death. I developed a pulmonary embolism—blood clots in my lungs—from an operation to repair a broken hip from a ski accident. But this time I was ready to be conscious and in a state of deep meditation. And while I didn't die, I felt I was much better prepared and actively engaged in meditation as death seemed close at hand.**

The combination of these two near-death experiences changed my life irreversibly, causing me to be more present, grateful, considerate, and loving. Since then, I have treated each day as if it could be my last, and I have tried to live fully into each moment of my life. I have found that preparing for death has actually

---

* These stories are described in more detail in Edward W. Bastian and Tina Staley, *Living Fully Dying Well*, ed. Netanel Miles-Yépez, Boulder, Colorado: Sounds True, 2009, which also includes material from Rabbi Zalman Schachter-Shalomi, Dr. Ira Byock, Dr. Marilyn Schlitz, Roshi Joan Halifax, Mother Tessa Bielicki, and Mirabai Starr.

helped me to live more fully, to be more loving, to treasure my relationships, and be grateful that I can both witness and finish what I was supposed to do in this life.

For the most part, my own view of death has been shaped by Buddhism, which has helped me to understand that I am a conscious being whose life-stream does not end with the physical death of our body. While my conceptual and perceptual activities are tied to the brain and nervous system, my conscious awareness is not. There are non-physical aspects of it that are not dependent on the body. This aspect of my consciousness exists like an ever-changing river, living on forever, and endlessly reshaping itself into physical life-forms and environments that reflect its inner qualities. After the physical death of this body, my consciousness will go into a dream-like state where it will experience a variety of temporary dream rebirths until it finally incarnates into a physical form where it will experience another cycle of birth and death.

The Sufi injunction, "Die before you die," exhorts us to extinguish our false sense of self, before death, to let go of our ego, our pride, our grasping, our anger, and our ignorance. It encourages us to live into the existence of our true nature, our ultimate identity with God, *Allah*. While Buddhism does not propose realization of our identity with God as the goal of spiritual practice like Sufi Islam and many other traditions, it does provide many practices to help us eliminate the negative *karma* caused by our ignorance, desire and anger. Once these are eliminated, or 'healed,' then we can be internally liberated, wise, loving, and tranquil amidst the cacophony of life around us. We can be reborn, both in this life and the next, in a positive realm of being.

Buddhism teaches that the final moments in the dying process hold great power for immediate spiritual transformation, potentially helping one to become an enlightened being, capable of returning to the world to help relieve the suffering of others. At the moment when all concepts and senses cease, and when the heat and consciousness of the body has withdrawn into the 'heart chakra' or center, there is a singular moment of bliss and clear light when the divine potential of the mind can fully manifest. It is in that moment that we can achieve enlightenment and liberation from the endless incarnations of birth and rebirth.

Tibetan Yogis, for example, carefully prepare for this moment by bringing themselves right up to the point of death in their meditations. They practice withdrawing consciousness into the heart chakra and central channel from which, at the end of their physical life, they can launch themselves to a heavenly realm of a Buddha to achieve full enlightenment in preparation for their eternal career of helping others to do the same.

Although I am not nearly as accomplished as these great yogis, this is the type of scenario I had hoped for in my own death, and it is why I was disappointed that I had nearly died with only consciousness of blackness and voidness. But reassuringly, this state of near-death consciousness is an integral part of the process described by Buddhism:

> When blackness arises, you will fall unconscious in the universal ground.
>
> Then the right life forces arise again and unconsciousness will fade away.
>
> At that time, the original brightness of the primordial state will arise.
>
> It is clear and unceasing, like the autumn sky.
>
> You remain in emptiness and clarity, free from the obscurations and coverings.*

While sitting on the emergency room gurney, recalling my own death, all I could remember was the blackness. But it wasn't non-existence; it was conscious awareness of the blackness. According to the Buddhist theory of death, this blackness marks the penultimate stage of life, the one that precedes the blissful clear light of death and the departure of consciousness from the body into the dream-like state of the *bardo*, the mental state of being that bridges the gap between this life and the next.

So it seems that my experience of the post-blackness stage of dying will have to await my next death. Then, if I am able, I'll return to tell you about it! But the truth is, it is probably impossible to gather enough evidence, and to conduct the kinds of double-blind studies required to achieve scientific certainty that consciousness survives the death of our bodies. However, there is an enormous body of anecdotal evidence that points to the survival and the possible reincarnation of consciousness. Therefore, from a purely

---

* Tulku Thondup, *Peaceful Death, Joyful Rebirth,* 50.

practical standpoint, it makes sense to me to live my life with the assumption that my consciousness will live on and to conduct my life accordingly. Living a compassionate and contemplative life is simply a wise investment for all the possible scenarios that may arise in the future.

So I encourage you to begin journaling about your own views on death. Include your fears, questions, doubts, hopes and dreams. Then look at death as an extraordinary opportunity to grow in wisdom, compassion and gratitude for each day of life. Death is our personal deadline for completing our life's mission. We just don't know when it will happen!

Don't wait until it's too late.

EXISTENCE

Is there a beginning or end to existence?
How and why do I exist? Did life evolve, or was it originally
created by a pre-existing God or divine force? What is the
relationship between consciousness and existence?

THERE IS A WONDROUS VARIETY of creation stories among the world's religions to explain our existence. People everywhere have always wondered how we and the universe came into being and if it will end. Spiritual traditions pass down creation stories about cosmic eggs or oceans, omnipotent gods and mythic couples, fantastic animals and magical purveyors of a grand illusion. Some stories say that each of us is the creator of our own universe. Others tell us that the world is just a projection of our own imagination and our unique blend of virtuous and non-virtuous qualities, wisdom and ignorance, selfishness and compassion.

Our personal views of the beginning and end of existence are subtly reflected in the way we live our lives. These views affect the ways in which we take responsibility for shaping our lives and improving the quality of the world around us. For example, if we believe that our thoughts and actions are known and predestined by a universal creator, as some do, it is possible then we might take less responsibility for own actions, having less compassion for others and taking little interest in making the world a better place.

In the Mandala Process we explore the various stories and explanations for the beginning and end of existence, and a context for discussing such questions as:

Is there a beginning or end to existence? Does there need to be a beginning for the universe to exist? If so, how did it begin? Does existence need to end? If so, how? If not, why? How do these answers affect the development of my spiritual path and my actions in the world?

MY OWN EXPERIENCE WITH THE QUESTION OF EXISTENCE

The Buddhist story of existence is quite different from the one I grew up with, that nothing existed until God created the world in seven days. In some ways, the Buddhist story has a lot in common with the science of modern physics that has yet to find the physical limits of the universe in time and space.

I understand the Buddhist story in the following ways: Existence is simply eternal and has no beginning or end. Universes implode and explode; the material objects that populate the universe are created by infinitely divisible particles. All objects in the universe are impermanent and interdependent, linked in a web of intricate and endless causality.

One of these elements (so to speak) of the universe is consciousness. By that I mean the capacity of all life-forms to be aware. In so far as our bodies are composed of the particles of the universe, we are a part of the universe that is aware of itself, i.e., the manifestation of the universe being aware of itself. Our consciousness does not exist independently of the material elements in the universe. Rather, it is an integral aspect of the interdependent matrix of existence. Therefore, consciousness is not an independent, free-standing, first-cause of the material universe. Rather, it is always flowing, changing, interacting and integrating with the material and energetic forces in the universe.

According to Buddhism and Hinduism, the capacity for conscious awareness is connected to, but not independently caused by, a subtle form of breath-energy that is called *prana* in Sanskrit. Riding together, conscious awareness and subtle breath-energy provide a necessary condition for all forms of life. For example, human life begins with the conjoining of a sperm and an egg along with consciousness riding on its constant companion, *prana*, the animating element of life.

Consciousness, therefore, is neither physical nor caused solely by physical bodies. But like a river, consciousness does carry with it the causal elements of its past history. These stored elements are called *karma*, for they quite literally make the future based on the experiences of the past. Therefore, when consciousness incarnates into a new human body, it carries with it all the predispositions and propensities from its past. These shape the human personality, emotions, perceptual lenses, and ways of being in relationship with other living beings.

Therefore, even though consciousness isn't the sole cause of physical existents, and physical existents aren't the sole cause of consciousness, it is impossible to consider them as totally separate and independent from one another. They are interdependently intertwined and one doesn't exist without the other.

Human consciousness doesn't merely reflect the realities perceived through sight, sound, smell, taste, and touch. It isn't just a passive bystander in the flow of life; for, based on karmic propensities accumulated from the past, human consciousness also projects its own way of viewing and interpreting the sensory data it receives. In this sense, the existence of the world is partly shaped by our own imagination.

From the Buddhist perspective, the infinite universe is populated with an infinite variety of conscious life-forms. Many of these may be beyond our capacity to perceive. Each of these beings has its own consciousness continuum. Like the river whose flow, shape and color reflect the lands through which is has traveled, the life form of these conscious beings reflect the quality of *karma* from its past lives. Their lives can be pleasant or unpleasant, depending on their accumulated 'good' or 'bad' *karma*. Beings of similar karmic propensities are drawn together to co-create the realms they inhabit.

The Buddhist universe is comprised of three major realms of life-forms. These are called the Form Realm, the Formless Realm, and the Desire Realm. Taken together, they comprise the whole of *Samsara* (literally, 'continuous flow'), a name given to the condition of life shaped by the *karma* from previous lives.

As human beings, we live in the desire realm. Together, we have co-created this form of earthy existence because of the similarities of our karmic propensities. Our bodies, sensory organs and minds have been formed, as it were, by our 'spiritual genes' or *karma*. In this realm of existence, nearly every thought and action is predicated on desire. We can observe this basic truth of human existence in our daily lives. Because of our desire for things we want, and our aversion to things we don't want, our moods and emotions shift constantly, leaving us in a state of continual mental turmoil. So long as we are ruled by attraction and aversion, we will be imprisoned by desire. We are driven by our desires. When we don't get what we want, we become impatient and agitated. This leads to anger, jealousy, hatred, and conflict. The Buddha was interested in how to break this cycle of desire, attachment, and all the negative emotions that flow from our ignorance of the true nature of reality. He wanted to help us become free from the endless cycles of rebirth in the suffering existence call *Samsara*.

Buddhism proposes that we are born here in this life-form to experience the results of our past karmic influences. We are here together, to play our respective dramatic roles, to learn the realities of life, and to transform our consciousness for the better. The human incarnation is an ideal platform for becoming enlightened and liberated. For, in this human form, we experience enough suffering to see its pervasive reality, we have the intelligence to determine the cause and the cure, and we have the mental capacity to engage in radical transformation. Therefore, the Buddha taught the Six Perfections as the vehicle to liberation. These are the Perfections of Generosity, Conduct, Patience, Perseverance, Meditation, and Wisdom. He also taught the so-called Four Seals, which are: all causal phenomena are impermanent; all phenomena are empty; all beings afflicted by ignorance will suffer; and *Nirvana* is peace.

From the Buddhist perspective, the goal of spiritual practice is to purify and eliminate the karmic causes that have imprisoned us in *Samsara*, and to develop a compassionate wisdom that will liberate us from suffering altogether. In our meditations, we can calm and focus our minds, we can gain insight into the ultimate nature of reality, we can experience the states of being of living beings in all the realms of existence, we can gain the power to liberate ourselves and others from the endless rounds of suffering. Blissfully liberated from within, we can then work eternally for the well-being of others.

This is simply my own personal experience and understanding of the nature of existence from a Buddhist perspective, and how this has impacted my own spiritual development. As with the other chapters in this book, I am offering it to you with the hope that you will begin journaling about your own spiritual answers and styles as they pertain to the formation of your personal spiritual path.

FREEDOM

Is it possible to be free from the struggles of normal life?
What would total freedom look like? How can I be free?

THE ASPIRATION FOR FREEDOM seems to be hard-wired into the human consciousness. While we recognize that we are bound and constrained by our bodies, our society, and our environment, we still dream of a state where we are free of these earthly limitations.

Our sense of freedom is relative to the condition in which we find ourselves. The abused spouse, the starving child, the political prisoner, the terminally ill patient and the homeless all share the intense desire to be free of the horrid chains that bind them to their condition. The adolescent child seeks freedom from parental control, the angry slave seeks freedom from an oppressive master, the repressed poet seeks freedom of expression, the dedicated teacher seeks freedom in the classroom, the itinerant farm worker seeks freedom from national borders, the ambitious capitalist seeks freedom from governmental intervention. We all aspire in our own ways to be free.

In the spiritual context, we seek the freedom to find our own path, a path that suits our own unique needs and predispositions. Once we are on the spiritual path, we desire nothing less than to achieve the liberation from negative emotions, freedom from ignorance and emancipation from suffering. We may even yearn for the wisdom to free others from the causes of their suffering.

The Spiritual Paths Mandala helps us to explore the meanings and promises of freedom from a broad variety of spiritual traditions. It helps us to investigate approaches to such questions as:

What is freedom? How can I be free? Can I control my destiny? Does the karma of my previous thoughts and actions pre-determine my future? How can I purify past wrongs so that I can become free?

My Own Experience with the Question of Freedom

In America, we are constantly bombarded by the claim that America is the Land of the Free. Here we proclaim the inalienable rights for 'freedom from tyranny,' 'freedom to vote,' 'sexual freedom,' 'freedom of the press,' 'freedom of the marketplace,' 'freedom of self governance,' 'freedom of equality,' 'freedom of religion,' and 'freedom to be happy.' Of all these freedoms, the 'freedom to be happy' was always the most perplexing to me as I was growing up. For amidst all the other freedoms, the 'freedom to be happy' was the most elusive. While all the other freedoms pertain to our external relationship with others in society, this last one, the 'freedom to be happy' is uniquely personal and internal.**

When I was young and leaving my Iowa home, one of the freedoms I most valued was the freedom to travel the world. I was free to explore the world's cultures, different ways of life and religions. As a hitchhiker through Europe, Africa, and Asia, I was picked up by an extraordinary variety of people, rich and poor, who took me into their homes and allowed me to experience their lives. In my brief stint with the Civil Rights movement in Alabama and Mississippi, I came in contact with freedom fighters who struggled for political, economic, and social equality. As a film-maker, I documented the religions of Asia and the effects of religion on the lives of ordinary people. As a photographer, I documented the war in Viet Nam. As a Buddhist scholar and practitioner, I lived in India among impoverished refugees from Tibet.

One of the most striking conclusions I made after having all of these experiences is that there is no direct correlation between external freedom or economic circumstance and internal happiness. I have witnessed people in pain and poverty with no apparent economic, political, and social freedom, who have inner lives of peace, contentment and empathy. Happiness, I discovered, is the result of inner freedom from the causes that bind and imprison us. This fact doesn't alleviate the need and responsibility to struggle for external freedoms; but, in our struggles, we need to be cognizant of the fact that inner freedom and happiness do not

---

* This is a simplification based on a common misunderstanding. The actual words in The Declaration of Independence are more subtle: "We hold these truths to be self-evident, that all men are created equal, that they are endowed by their Creator with certain unalienable Rights, that among these are Life, Liberty and the pursuit of Happiness."

automatically arise because we experience external freedom and prosperity.

I first heard this message from an unlikely source. It happened as I was headed to Viet Nam to experience and document the war as a free-lance photographer. Ironically, America's rationale for the oppressive war was to liberate the Vietnamese people from the threat of Communism. Perhaps the most tragic phrase of the war was, "We had to destroy the village to free them from the Viet Cong."

I had landed in Bangkok, Thailand, where I was waiting for a flight to Saigon the next day. So I was free to wander the streets and clubs that night. It was in one of these clubs that I met a couple of young Thai women who invited me to join them on the dance floor. And, of course, being a young, red-blooded male, I obliged them. After about an hour, one of them asked me if I would like to go home with her. Now, I had heard about the rampant prostitution in Bangkok, which drew many tourists and soldiers there, but I wasn't interested. So I was just about the decline the young woman's offer when she said, "I am not a prostitute. I was married to an American soldier who was killed in Viet Nam and I would just like your company." That was different. I agreed, and off we went to her apartment nearby.

In the morning, after a lovely night together, she told me that her father was on his way over for breakfast. With that, I suggested it was time for me to go, but she begged me to stay, saying, it was important for me to meet him. So we sat together in the kitchen savoring a cup of tea and waiting for his arrival. Within a few minutes, we heard a gentle knock at the door and in walked a diminutive Buddhist monk, her father. He was so warm and friendly that I was immediately at ease in his company. His questions to me were translated by his daughter, and soon, I was asking him questions about Buddhism.

So it was in that small Bangkok kitchen that I received my first teachings on Buddhism, teachings about how we can achieve real freedom. He explained to me that material things and sensual experiences could not make me happy, that my happiness and freedom must come from within. "So long as we believe happiness will come from outside, we will be unhappy and imprisoned by this delusion," he said. Then he told me about the Four Noble Truths, which encapsulate all the Buddha's teachings. These are:

All beings are in a state of suffering; Our suffering is caused by our ignorance, desire, and anger; Freedom from suffering is possible; the practices of wisdom and compassion can eliminate these internal causes of suffering, enable us to be free and to free others from suffering.

I have to admit, as a young man who had just enjoyed an unexpectedly wonderful night with his daughter, these teachings presented me with quite a challenge. But I revered this simple monk and his wisdom. And somehow, deep inside, I knew they were true. Still, I wasn't quite ready to give up my illusion of external freedom and happiness.

Over the years that followed, his wisdom continued to work on me; and once I had learned (through much experimentation) that material and sensual experiences could not make me happy, I was increasingly drawn to the Buddhist perspective. Thus, I began my Buddhist studies to find an inner path to happiness.

Perhaps the most striking thing about the Buddhist view is that internal freedom emerges naturally when we remove the chains of bondage to our material and sensual attachments. In other words, we focus on removing the *causes* rather than accumulating the results. Inner freedom comes through emptying ourselves of our negative propensities which produce negative emotions like greed, anger and jealousy. It is a subtractive process more than an additive one. This path leads us to live simply with what we really need, rather than what we want.

The process for internal freedom begins with knowledge that our "self" is not a permanent independent unit that is separate from others. This knowledge of selflessness must be both intellectually understood and meditatively experienced. It is the truth of our interdependence with all other beings and the environment in which we live. It is the truth of universal reciprocity between all forms of life. It is a genuine empathy for others, knowing that our well-being is intertwined with theirs.

When our sensual and materialistic activities are tempered by this knowledge and a direct experience of interdependence and empathy, we don't engage our desires with the expectation that they will cause lasting happiness. This knowledge in turn lessens our desire, craving, grasping, and dependence on external stimulation for internal well-being. We become free of this illusion and content through internal equanimity.

Over the years, I have found meditation to be an important tool for fulfilling my freedom to be happy, and I have adapted classical Buddhist techniques for this purpose. The underlying assumption, of course, is that our minds have the natural capacity to be in a state of peace, tranquility and equanimity when the causes of unhappiness have been healed and removed. Sometimes, my meditation on emptiness and interdependence focuses on the actual unhappy emotion I am feeling. Through this meditation, the negative emotion is transformed into a feeling of equanimity and contentment. This meditation can be practiced at any time and in any place. It enables me to be internally free from external attractions.

I begin by simply being mindful of my attraction to, or repulsion from external sensory stimuli. I observe this feeling objectively, without passing judgment on it. For example, I observe how a negative feeling causes pain or stiffness in my head, neck, back or stomach, and notice how this single negative feeling can set off a chain of emotional reactions like anger and depression. Sometimes, the unpleasant physical sensation draws my attention to a precipitating emotional cause. Then I put this negative emotional cause under my mental microscope to discover what it is made of and what precipitated it.

For example, it might arise from my fear of having too little money to support myself in my old age. It might be the result of my unfulfilled desire for a partner, a soul-mate to accompany me through the next phase in my life. It might arise from my worry about my children and other family members. Without judging or rejecting this emotion, I examine what caused the negative emotion and realize that it is my unrealistic expectation that money, relationships or my children's well-being could be the sole cause of my happiness.

From a Buddhist perspective, I meditate on the impermanence of relationships, and how they are empty of the inherent capacity to create happiness. I empty myself of the false projections I have unconsciously formed about potential partners. I remind myself of the interdependence of all things, and that my well-being is dependent on the well-being of others with whom I am in relationship.

Thus, my personal antidote for dealing with a negative emotion is the following:

1. Objectively and dispassionately observe the negative emotion.

2. Focus attention on breathing to pacify the secondary mental and physiological effects of this emotion (the breathing will create a gap between the stimulus of desire and the response to it).

3. Examine the cause of the unhappy emotion and see that it is an unrealistic expectation that an external thing, sensation, or relationship can cause me to be happy.

4. Focus on the impermanence and emptiness of desires, projections, and the unhappiness they create (this, along with the breathing, allows the effects of the emotion to dissipate).

5. Realize that both oneself and all objects of perception are empty of inherent existence.

6. Experience the mental equanimity that arises from gentle breathing, and from pacifying a desire based on false expectations.

7. Allow the natural state of equanimity, contentment, peace and happiness to rise up and enjoy that feeling within.

8. Remember that even this equanimity is interdependent and refrain from attachment to it.

9. Replace the unhappy emotion with a compassionate intention to become enlightened in order to liberate others from the causes of their suffering.

In this way, every unhappy emotion can become an object of meditation and can be healed, thus allowing our internal state of happiness to emerge. Gradually, Buddhist meditation frees us from external desires and liberates us through internal contentment. This meditation does not negate the importance for compassionate engagement with others, but it quells the self-centered projections that create unhappiness when other people or things fail to live up to our false projections and expectations of them.

This type of meditation can be practiced on all negative emotions—such as greed, jealousy, anger or hatred—that arise from unhealthy desires and attachment—to money, possessions or relationships. When we apply this meditation successfully, our minds are released from the suffering of desire and can reside in a quiescent state of internal happiness and freedom.

The result is freedom from the causes of suffering. This inner freedom enables us to fully engage the vicissitudes of daily life, to help relieve the suffering of others, and to work for social and environmental justice. Unburdened by attachment to false promises of external freedom, we are thus liberated from within and can live lives of compassionate equanimity.

God

*Is there a universal creator or divine
creative energy behind all that exists?
If so, what is it? What is God?*

QUESTIONS ABOUT THE EXISTENCE of God seem to have been with human beings forever. It is rare to find someone, anywhere, who has not experienced either the comfort of God, the pain of God's absence, or the dilemma of questioning God's existence.

Throughout the world, there are many points of view about the existence of God. Some say that even the idea of God would be impossible if God didn't actually exist. They explain that the beauty, the harmony, the design, and even the very existence of the universe would be impossible without a divine creator. Others say that God is merely a product of a human need for a universal parent, protector and creator. They explain that 'God' is created by us, in our own image, and in response to our own needs and capacities.

Some people report that they have directly experienced God, *the Divine Being,* existing beyond the limitations of the five senses. To demonstrate this, they offer the eloquence of their testimony, the inspiration of their art, or their own living examples as evidence of a profound experience with Divinity.

There are many who simply dwell in the belief in God, because no other explanation is satisfying; no other relationship fills the void of existential loneliness. On the other hand, there are atheists who simply cannot believe in God, because the existence of such a being seems to them, irrational. And in between there are the agnostics who can't make up their minds, who are waiting to be convinced one way or the other.

In many cultures, divine beings or deities are 'felt' just beyond the veil of worldly appearances and 'sensed' amid every aspect of the nature. There are many others who believe that the word 'God' actually stands for the wholeness of all existence, that is to say, the ineffable mystery behind all that is. There are apophatic mystics who feel that any attempt to describe or name this mystery will merely push God further away, hiding divinity from the possibility of human connection.

The mere fact of human individuality requires each person to understand, to experience, and to describe God or the Ultimate Reality according to her own unique life-experience and spiritual style. The Spiritual Paths Mandala is designed to stimulate and point our exploration toward the wide variety of meanings and opinions about God.

MY OWN EXPERIENCE WITH THE QUESTION OF GOD

As a child, I had problems with idea of God, even though my church and my parents had instructed me in the basic prayers, commandments, and scriptures. Though, in times of trouble, I turned to God for help in prayer, my youthful attempts at faith were always overwhelmed with questions:

If God is good and all-powerful, why does he allow bad things to happen? If God created the universe, where did God come from? If God takes the side of the Christians, and only lets them into heaven, what happens to everyone else? If God created the Earth and all the species in seven days, what about the science of evolution?

As a young man brought up in the Presbyterian Church, I heard nothing about the mystical, non-dual approaches to Christianity. I hadn't been exposed to the works of Christian mystics like Meister Eckhardt, Mechthild of Magdeburg, Teresa of Avila, and St. John of the Cross. So I was burdened by the image of God as a powerful old man with a white beard as depicted on the ceiling of the Sistine Chapel in Rome.

But I have since learned that Christians, Muslims, Jews, Native Americans and Hindus have much more nuanced conceptions and experiences of God than I was able to recognize and understand as a child. Ironically, my study of Buddhism has helped me see Christianity in a whole new light. Perhaps, if I were exposed to these mystical writings earlier, my search would have led me deeper into the tradition of my birth instead of to an ancient religion from Asia.

While I was comfortable with many of the ethical principles of Christianity, I was very uncomfortable with the idea of God, as well as the institutional opposition to women clergy, homosexuality, and birth control I saw in the Church. So I began to look at other religions to see how they dealt with the knotty question of God, while still retaining other ethical features like the Golden Rule that I found essential and rational.

The traditions that were most comfortable for me were Buddhism and Taoism, as both seemed to offer a deep spiritual practice without the dogmatic beliefs in God (as I understood 'Him' to be) that I found so objectionable. When life circumstances led me to Buddhism, I felt a great sense of relief that I could have a spiritual practice that wasn't based on faith in something I couldn't justify rationally.

Buddhism addressed my basic questions about the existence of a 'Creator.' If the creator god had no cause for its own existence, Buddhism suggested, such a god would be inert, static, permanent, and unchangeable. Therefore, such a God would be outside the realm of causality and couldn't bring anything into existence.

Buddhism explains that it is our limited perceptual capacity and faulty thinking that compels us to seek a first cause (i.e., creator God) for our existence. Buddhism argues that this idea cannot be supported either logically or empirically. Therefore, Buddhists accept the proposition that existence and individual consciousness (i.e., impermanent soul) has no beginning or end, and that a creator God isn't necessary for things to exist.

Many people today make the following kinds of statements about the world's religions:

All religions believe in the same God, but have different names for it. All religions begin from the same source and lead people to the same goal.

This hope for a single Truth for all religions and peoples is understandable. Those who propose it often believe that world peace would be easier if all the religions of the world worshiped the same God, all united in the Oneness of a single divine Creator. Yet this strategy for peace around a One God has not worked out very well. Perhaps it is because it is impossible for everyone to believe in exactly the same thing at the same time. Perhaps the idea of God varies according to the state of mind of each person who believes. Perhaps it is because humans are simply too diverse in our stages evolution and our unique combination of archetypal styles to all define God in the same way. Perhaps it is because a one-size-fits-all belief in God simply won't work for all people at all times. Perhaps it is because God is beyond words, description, and even human imagination and, therefore, impossible to be the organizing principle for world peace.

Perhaps the only way to define God is to describe what God is not, and to empty-out all our mental preconceptions of what God might be. Perhaps the notion of Oneness, as wonderful as it seems, brings with it an unintended consequence of divisiveness, simply because of the limitations and diversity of human minds.

But there might be an alternative strategy to Oneness as a vehicle for world peace. This strategy would celebrate diversity, rather than Oneness. It would engender a love of diversity, rather than imposing worship of the One. It would simply appreciate and celebrate the marvelous multiplicity of loving spiritual beliefs and practices.

I sometimes surmise that if there were a God who set the creation of the universe in motion, that He-She-It would be enthralled by the vibrant diversity of all the life in this creation. Perhaps God would even be a little amused by the myriad of diverse spiritual beliefs and practices that humans have created to explain their own existence. Perhaps this God would not be looking in the mirror with an attitude of self-glorification, but rather would take greater pleasure in gazing lovingly at all of creation. Perhaps God would prefer us to focus our love on each other rather than heaping praise and devotion on Him-Her-It! Perhaps God would encourage us to celebrate, honor, love, and protect the marvelous diversity of life. Perhaps we might find peace, harmony and unity through our love of diversity rather than blind obedience to God.

It seems to me, that if there is just one God that is the divine creative force in the universe, it cannot be known through our names or descriptions, for it's existence is beyond the capacities of knowledge by our limited mental faculties. Therefore, I am fond of the apophatic practices of the Hesychasts, the emptiness practices of Buddhism, the beginningless universal flow of the

Taoists, and the not-naming G-d convention of Judaism. It is through the emptying-out of names, concepts and beliefs that our consciousness expands and melds into the holistic unknowingness of our infinite existence.

I am aware that I have been something of a thorn in the side of my God-oriented friends and fellow teachers in dialogues. I am always kidding them about God (and they do the same with me about emptiness). While they are comfortable with the term, I still am not. Each person has their own unique understanding of God, and there is no single God that we all agree on. Reifying the divine, I believe, only pushes it away. Still, they are all patient with me. After all, I am just a Buddhist!

Yet as we (my friends and fellow teachers) meditate and pray together, each with our own way of being or not-being with God, I feel a profound and sublime unity in our experience with each other and that which we call sacred. So it has become clear to me that when joined in contemplative love and quiescence, the word God doesn't matter. This shared spiritual experience, it seems to me, is the foundation for true and lasting peace on earth.

GOOD & EVIL

What is 'the good'? Do I need to be good to be happy?
What does it mean to be a 'good person'? Are there
countervailing forces of good and evil in the world?

THE STUDY OF THE 'GOOD' entails an examination of the ethical quality and intention of our thoughts, actions and words, and the methods we employ to achieve happiness, health and wealth. Ethics is the branch of knowledge that can help us to utilize our body, mind and speech in service of 'the Good' for other people, the environment, as well as our own happiness.

Since happiness is the common goal of all people, the idea of the 'Good' generally, and ethics specifically, might be described as a science for helping people to become happy.

The spiritual traditions of the world all provide ethical and moral teachings about what is good. Spiritual practices are designed to help people achieve happiness, peace and well-being in this life and in the next. These teachings and practices advise people not to lie, steal, kill, slander or cause harm to others. They provide methods for cultivating love, compassion, kindness and wisdom.

The principles guiding ethical behavior assume that there is a cause and effect relationship between each person's past thoughts, actions and words, and their future happiness. Simply put, good behavior leads to happiness and contentment and bad behavior leads to sadness and turmoil.

Therefore, spiritual development cannot be separated from ethical conduct. Good ethics lead to a tranquil and peaceful state of mind, making it easier to meditate, contemplate, pray, perform rituals and engage in devotional practice. Good ethics help the mind to become clear and pure, preparing it for the transmigration from one life to the next. In return, good meditation helps us to be good and wise human beings.

The Spiritual Paths Mandala provides a context for a multi-traditional study and conversation about 'the Good,' and the exploration of such related questions as:

Is there one set of ethics that holds for all humanity? Are ethics relative to one's time, place, culture, ethnicity and circumstances? Is there such a thing as evil? Do you have to be 'good' to be happy? How are good behavior and spiritual realization interrelated?

MY OWN EXPERIENCE WITH THE QUESTION OF 'THE GOOD'

"Be a good boy, Eddie," my mother used to tell me. Those words always rang in my ears as I struggled to obey them. To me, 'being good' meant doing what I was told, following the rules, cleaning my room, finishing my dinner, getting good grades, avoiding sex before marriage and alcohol before I was twenty-one, winning the game, but also being a good sport when I lost. Being a "good boy" is what was required to gain praise, approval and love. Not being good meant criticism and punishment. Not that my parents were mean or unusually strict or harsh. They weren't . . . they were wonderful people who just wanted me to be an accepted and successful member of society. And they wanted my good behavior to reflect well on our whole family.

To me, being 'good' in the rule-bound society of that time meant the same as *not being myself* and *not having any fun!* Being 'good' meant constant regulation and restriction under the watchful and critical eye of parents, teachers and coaches. There was little room for spontaneity. Yet, growing up, I could see the hypocrisy in the adults around me who often broke the same rules they were enforcing. When I asked why they weren't practicing what they preached, I was instructed: "Do what I say, not what I do." As a young person trained for leadership in society, I learned that pretending to follow the rules was more important than actually following them.

It seemed to me that I was being encouraged to become a lawyer, an accountant, or a politician, so that I could write and manipulate laws that would work in the favor of my own socio-economic class. But I could see that these faulty adult strategies for being 'good' were not making them happy.

Nevertheless, as a 'good son' of my society, I pretended to do what they said. But as a 'true son' of my society, I also did what they did in secret. Thus, my friends and I found ways to break the rules in clever ways that kept us from getting caught. You had to look like you were following the rules while hiding the bad things you were doing. And the pay-off seemed worth it. Being surreptitiously bad meant that you could have a better house, car and food, gain tactical advantage in school, business, politics, and sports, all without sacrificing the vices that made certain things easier and more pleasurable. You could beat-out other guys for a girl by looking good on the outside while being slightly bad on the inside. 'All is fair in love and war,' we were told. We found that looking good while doing bad confuses people and gives you time to complete your scheme before you're caught and can move on.

This is the mind-set that leads to pyramid schemes in business, where you lie about the value of your business, getting others to invest in it and taking their money before the whole enterprise goes belly up. So long as you look good while doing the shady things that benefit your allies, they will turn a blind eye to the rest of our life. Life was a theater, and the trick was not to get caught out of costume, not acting your part! This was the illusory strategy I learned for happiness and success.

The word 'good' is one of the most commonly used words in all languages: 'Be good!' 'Have a good time.' 'Think good thoughts!' Even the knee-jerk response to the question, 'How are you?' is simply 'Good!' That happy and confident response often hides the suppressed fear and anxiety that accompanies much of our life.

The real meaning of the word 'good' lies somewhere on a sliding scale that measures the quality of everything we think, say and do. At one end of the scale is the word 'bad,' or even 'evil.' At the other end is the word 'good' or even 'perfect.' The color at the 'bad end' is black, and the color at the 'good end' is white. In between is a sliding gradation of gray, whose tone is lighter or darker depending on the relative mixture of good and bad. At the black end sits the devil, and at the white end sits God. The black end yields eternal damnation and misery, and the white end yields eternal happiness and bliss. In between the two is a soupy mixture of both. Since most of us live somewhere along that sliding scale of relative grayness, our lives are a constant mixture of contentment and turmoil.

But what are the ingredients of bad and good, and why do they make us feel sad or happy? How do we look inside ourselves and determine where we are along that scale? Each of the world's religions, along with great philosophers like Socrates and Plato, provide criteria for this judgment. They provide a coherent rationale linking wisdom, goodness, and happiness. They offer codes that we can live by that set the ground rules for preventing violence, greed, and the mayhem that results from unregulated self-interest:

Do not kill, steal, lie, commit adultery, or covet another's possessions. Love your neighbor as your self. Be generous, kind, patient, steadfast, focused, and wise. Eat properly, care for your animals, preserve your land, and do not degrade the environment. Do not worship the idols of fame and fortune over the divine truths and ethical codes of your spiritual tradition.

These moral codes of word, thought and action are at the heart of every religion.

The enduring challenge for us as human beings is to discover the means of cultivating happiness and success in a dog-eat-dog world while still seeking answers to these questions:

How can I do well by doing good? How can I love and take care of others, while still looking after 'number one'? How can I define 'the good' in such a way that being good is a winning strategy for happiness? What is 'the good' anyway?

In Buddhism, any thought, word or action is 'good' if it is motivated by love, compassion, empathy and kindness, along with wisdom that sees the interdependent nature of all things. Love is the sincere wish for the happiness of another being. Compassion is the sincere intention to remove the causes of their suffering. 'Great Compassion' *(mahakaruna)* is the vow to become enlightened in order to liberate all beings from suffering. This loving and compassionate intention resonates with the intentions that Jesus also laid out for his followers: "Love your neighbor as yourself," and "do unto others as your would have them do unto you." Simply put, our own inner peace of mind arises when we wisely seek to help others.

Here, the emphasis is placed on the inner intention, rather

than the actual the physical word or action. For sometimes wise and well-intentioned stern words and tough actions are the best medicine. An extreme example can be found in the story of a tenth century King of Tibet who is said to have banned Buddhism from Tibet in favor of the older indigenous Bön religion. Many Buddhist monks and lay people were banished or killed and monasteries were destroyed. To save the Tibetan people from the atrocities of that evil king, a Buddhist monk appeared at the winter festival disguised as a Bön sorcerer. He was riding a white horse that he had painted black just before he entered the courtyard. He then dismounted the horse, dazzling and entrancing the king with a dance, and then fatally stabbed him with a ceremonial sword. Then, leaping back onto his horse, he road out of the palace and crossed the nearest river where he threw away his costume, washed the black paint from his horse and escaped. With that daring, controversial, and arguably compassionate act, he saved Buddhism in Tibet and the lives of thousands of innocent people.

On the opposite end of the spectrum is the story of the Indian Buddhist monk named Asanga, who spent decades in solitary meditation in order to come face-to-face with Maitreya, the Buddha of the Future. In this story, Asanga who was nearing the end of his capacity to persevere, wandered out of his cave and discovered a dying dog lying on the path in front of him. The dog was emaciated, bleeding, and surely nothing could save its life. Nevertheless, Asanga knelt down to examine its wounds and saw that maggots were eating away at the dog's decaying flesh. Hoping to heal the open wound, Asanga realized that he would have to remove the maggots. But if he did so with his hands, he ran the risk of endangering the maggots' lives as well. So he lowered his face to the wound and began to remove the maggots one-by-one with his tongue! In that instant, the apparition of dog was replaced by the actual body of the Buddha, Maitreya. In the excitement of the moment, Asanga lifted Maitreya into the air and placed him on his shoulders and walked to the village. But as he walked along the path, the villagers only saw the dying dog lying across his shoulders (who was actually Maiteya in disguise)!

Like the story of Jesus Christ on the Cross, this story of Asanga illustrates the utter profundity and sublime magnificence of Great Compassion, providing us with strong archetypal images of selfless giving—the highest of all human aspirations. When we are good,

good things happen to us. This is the universal law of reciprocity.

In Buddhism, the idea of 'the good' emerges from an objective analysis of our futile attempts to find happiness and contentment through material possessions and sensual gratification. Contentment comes from internal goodness, not external acquisitions. Since goodness requires a foundation of mental equanimity, compassion and wisdom, and since happiness depends on goodness, therefore happiness also depends on equanimity, compassion and wisdom.

Making money by pretending to be 'good' only creates more mental turmoil—the opposite of contentment and equanimity. Happiness cannot be sustained by attachment to external things, experiences and relationships. Yet, the wonderful irony is that those same external things can be enjoyed even more if we approach them with love, compassion, and a wisdom that sees them as impermanent, interdependent phenomena, empty of the inherent capacity to make us happy.

Being good, therefore, is not what I thought it was as a child. It is not just a matter of conforming to the norms of society, to be pleasing in the eyes of others, and therefore, finding external happiness and success. Rather, being good is to dedicate everything we do and say with the intention of love, compassion, and wisdom. The relative quality of our goodness, and therefore, the quality of our happiness and contentment, is dependent on our compassionate intentions.

For Buddhism, the existence of 'evil' in the world does not present a metaphysical conundrum. For, unlike the Abrahamic traditions, Buddhism does not believe there is a creator God who is inherently good. Therefore, Buddhism doesn't have to wrestle with the question: why is there evil in the world if the world is created by a good and perfect God? For Buddhism, 'evil' is just the opposite of good. It is simply a term for extremely bad intentions and immoral thoughts, words and actions.

HAPPINESS

Is happiness the same as fun and enjoyment?
What is true happiness? And how do we achieve it?

HAPPINESS IS THE COMMON GOAL of all beings, and the thread that connects us all in shared, collective purpose. Our individual lives provide the workshop wherein each of us attempts to design our own version of personal happiness. Our relationships with others provide us with the testing-ground wherein our designs for happiness are proven either to succeed or to fail. Day after day, consciously or unconsciously, we work and rework our strategics for happiness. Beneath nearly everything we do resides the same question, 'Will this make me happy?'

Spiritual traditions provide methods and roadmaps to happiness. While they rarely promise complete happiness in this life, many offer methods for eternal happiness in the next. The spiritual wisdom and methods proposed are often arduous, though also occasionally blissful. Spiritual discipline promotes a sense of peace and well-being with the knowledge that one is proactively pursuing a long-term agenda of happiness.

The pursuit of happiness in the context of spirituality forces one to evaluate our normal strategies and designs for happiness. We are compelled to look at our lives with honesty and to examine our motivations for relationships with others. We examine our faulty strategies for amassing the material goods and the sensory objects that smell good, taste delicious, feel sensuous, look beautiful and sound soothing. We gradually recognize the false promise of the constant barrage of advertisements pushing us toward more and more seductive ways to be happy and feel great.

As we discover spiritual strategies for happiness, we begin to recognize the faulty designs we have endlessly been generating for worldly wealth, fame, sensory gratification and comfort. We see these as transient, temporary and fruitless. Gradually, we begin replacing these with the peace, tranquility and wisdom of spiritual practice.

The Mandala Process is to gather together strategies and designs for happiness provided by authentic teachers and exemplars of many spiritual traditions. We explore the many questions related to happiness including:

> *What is true happiness? How can I achieve it? What is the relationship between wisdom, goodness, and happiness? Is fulfilling one's 'duty' a prerequisite to happiness? Is happiness just fulfilling selfish desires? Is happiness dependent on being good or altruistic? How do spiritual traditions fulfill the need for happiness? How do I select the one that is right for me?*

MY OWN EXPERIENCE WITH THE QUESTION OF HAPPINESS

As I mentioned earlier, I have often thought of happiness in the context of America's Declaration of Independence, which begins with one of the most elegant and inspirational sentences ever written:

> We hold these truths to be self-evident, that all men are created equal, that they are endowed by their Creator with certain inalienable Rights, that among these are Life, Liberty and the pursuit of Happiness.

This Declaration of Independence has provided both an amazing opportunity and a daunting challenge to the citizens of this new nation. It was written in 1776 by men of Christian descent, who could hardly have foreseen the tremendous religious pluralism of America's future. And yet, their words laid a strong ethical foundation for what has become the most ethnically and religiously diverse country on the face of the earth.

Among these diverse religious traditions in America is Buddhism, whose three to four million American followers make up less than two percent of the total population. Yet, the influence of Buddhist aesthetics, principles and meditation practices can now be found throughout American culture.

If the Declaration of Independence were to have been written by Buddhists, it would have retained many of the same ethical and inspirational sentiments, but the metaphysical references would have been slightly different. In truth, these references probably don't matter much to most Buddhists today. But if we look at these words through classical Buddhist lenses, they might provide us with a good jumping off place to examine the Buddhist approach to happiness and its ways of achieving it.

First are the words in the title: "Declaration of Independence." Now this word, 'independence,' is a hot-button for Buddhist critique. Simply put, from a Buddhist perspective, no thing, person, or nation can be totally independent, i.e., free from the myriad of causes and influences that condition its very being. The Buddha emphasized that everything is in fact 'interdependent' and not 'independent.' No person (or country) can be aloof from the surrounding environmental, economic, political, and religious influences of others. This is especially 'self-evident' in today's globalization of international trade, immigration, travel, and the internet. Environmental pollution in one country affects the health and well-being of people throughout the globe. Over fishing in one part of the ocean creates food shortages and upsets the fragile web of life in oceans everywhere. Human rights abuses in one country create an outcry and retribution from other countries. Manufacturing in Asia fuels the economies of Europe and America. Religious ideas from Asia and the Middle East have become integral to the fabric of American culture and society. Therefore, from both the perspective of Buddhism and the global interdependence of the modern world, this founding American document might well be renamed The Declaration of InterDependence.

Another phrase that could be challenging from the Buddhist perspective is "endowed by their Creator." This is because Buddhists don't believe that the universe or individual beings owe their existence to an independent creator God. Rather, the existence of the universe and every living being has no beginning or end. The universe is infinitely long and expansive. The consciousness of every living being is eternal. Therefore, Buddhists do quite well without the belief in a "Creator."

The idea of God can be puzzling to Buddhists; for, there is such an amazing diversity of definitions and connotations of the single word, God, that the word itself can't convey all these possibilities. For example, there might be some fundamentalist Christians,

Jews, Muslims and Hindus, who envision God as a Universal Male Creator with direct power over our lives. On the other end of the spectrum, there might be others within the same religions who use the word God as a verbal designation for the dynamic, ever-changing Creative Energy of the Universe that none of us can fully comprehend. (And this connotation might be acceptable to many Buddhists.) Therefore, from a Buddhist perspective, these words "endowed by their Creator" might be changed to "endowed by Creation."

Next are the words ". . . with certain inalienable Rights, that among these are Life, Liberty and the pursuit of Happiness." For a Buddhist, the rights of life, liberty, and pursuit of happiness cannot be endowed by one being upon another. Rather, "life, liberty, and the pursuit of happiness" are simply built into the natural causality of human existence. "Life" is simply the existential capacity of every living being. "Liberty" is not a right to be granted; it is gained through the conscious intention, vigilance and effort of each individual to liberate themselves from both the external tyranny of others and the internal oppression of ignorance, attachment, and anger. "Happiness" is the contentment, equanimity, joy, and well-being that emerges from an internal life molded by the intentions of compassion, love, empathy, and the wisdom that directly perceives the interdependence of all things.

From a Buddhist perspective, happiness is caused by actualizing the principles embodied in the Eightfold Path. These are Right View, Right Intention, Right Speech, Right Action, Right Livelihood, Right Effort, Right Mindfulness, and Right Concentration. But happiness is also caused by eliminating the negative factors of the so-called three poisons: ignorance, attachment, and desire.

Ignorance is the mistaken belief that objects, sensations, and relationships can be the sole cause of our happiness or unhappiness. Attachment is the tendency to cling onto those things we desire with the erroneous belief that they can make us happy. Anger is the negative emotion that arises when we can't get the things we desire and when the things we desire don't make us happy. The antidote to these 'poisons' is a wisdom that sees the fallacy of this belief, meditation that frees our mind from the causes of attachment and anger, and compassion that seeks to alleviate the suffering of others who are clouded by the same delusion.

The underlying premise of Buddhism is that our minds have the natural capacity to be happy, to be liberated, and to enjoy the infinite possibilities of a life fully-lived. So, aside from these metaphysical references in the Declaration of Independence, the goals of Buddhism and of America's founding fathers are harmonious with one another. While the Declaration of Independence, the Bill of Rights, and the United States Constitution help provide the external causes and conditions for happiness, Buddhism, like the other great spiritual traditions now rooted in American soil, look after the internal causes for life, liberty and the pursuit of happiness. The First Amendment of the US Constitution assures freedom of religion; thus each citizen has the freedom to cultivate the inner causes of individual happiness as taught by the religion or ethical system of his or her choice.

REALITY

Does the world around me exist in the way I perceive it?
How much of the external world is created by my
own biases and projections?

"BEAUTY," IT IS SAID, "is in the eye of the beholder." The same might be said for 'reality,' especially in the context of which values are real and which are false. Here, the truly spiritual person will define 'real values' differently from a materialistic person who seeks immediate gratification from worldly objects and from wealth and power.

What is 'real,' therefore, can be determined by examining the psychological result of holding a materialistic set of values versus holding a spiritual set of values. The proof of what has 'real value,' is based on which set of values creates sustainable happiness.

For example, the materialist might say that money, sex, possessions and power have 'real value' because they create immediate gratification in this world. The spiritual person might counter that materialistic and sensual gratification have no real value because they only cause a short-term gratification that results in long-term misery.

The materialist might say that greed, envy, and selfishness are real values because they make the world go 'round, and they motivate us to get the things we need to make us successful. The spiritual person might counter that these emotions have no real value because they are the cause of endless craving and dissatisfaction.

A materialist might say that the objects of perception exist independently and cause us to perceive them as they are. The philosopher and scientist might reply that the objects we see also depend on the mind that perceives, names and describes them. The values we perceive in material objects are created by the mind.

The materialist might say that spiritual wisdom is irrelevant because it does not help us acquire the accoutrements of wealth, power and success. The spiritual person might counter that the only real values are wisdom and compassion because they alone have the potential to see things as they are and create eternal happiness for oneself and all beings.

In the Mandala Process one explores different explanations of reality and real values in the world according to various spiritual and secular wisdom traditions. Here, one probes answers to such questions as:

How are spiritual values better and more real than materialistic values? Is the world I see real or an illusion? Is it possible to know what is real and what is not? Why does an accurate view of reality matter for my happiness and spiritual transformation?

MY OWN EXPERIENCE WITH THE QUESTION OF REALITY

On the night of a full moon at Sera Buddhist Monastery in Southern India in the late 1970s, I stood outside sipping evening tea with a few of the monks who had recently escaped from Tibet. These monks had been schooled in the ancient cosmology of Buddhism and had very little exposure to modern astronomy and astrophysics.

I had recently picked up an old copy of *Time Magazine* that had a picture of Americans landing on the moon and I had just showed this picture to my Buddhist friends. They looked at it with puzzlement, disbelief and typical Tibetan humor. And now, as we stood together looking up at the bright full moon, one of the monks asked:

"So you think that Americans have gone to the moon, right?"

"Yes, that is right," I responded.

"What did they find there," he asked.

"The American astronauts reported that the moon was made of rocks and dust?

"Does it have its own source of light to make it visible?"

"No it doesn't," I replied.

"Then, how do we see it if it doesn't have its own light source?"

"We can see it because the sun illuminates it," I said.

"And you think that right now we are looking at the very same moon on which they landed?"

"Yep. They landed on the moon we are all looking at right now," I said.

With that answer, they all had a good chuckle.

"Why are you laughing?" I asked.

"It is because the moon we are looking at is made of crystal and it shines its own light so we can see it. Therefore, the Americans must have gone to another place they mistakenly called the moon. It is not the same place we are looking at right now."

These wonderful and intelligent Tibetan monks with whom I was living were born, raised, and educated beyond the Himalayan mountains and their culture had been isolated from the rest of the world for over a thousand years. So they were looking at the moon through eyes that had not been influenced by western physics and astronomy. They had missed the scientific revolution, and the industrial revolution, only to have their country ravaged by the Chinese Cultural Revolution. We were looking at the same thing, but because of our intellectual and cultural biases, its reality for each of us couldn't have been more different.

Yet, even though the ancient Buddhist description of the moon's reality differs from our modern understanding, it still has a valuable perspective to offer regarding the underlying nature of the moon. For example, a fundamentalist Christian might have a better explanation for the physical properties of the moon, but still might believe that it was ultimately created by the fiat of an external God. While the Buddhist might hold an inaccurate description of the moon's properties, they see the moon as part of an endlessly sophisticated and interdependent matrix of causes and conditions that brought it into existence. And this latter view is closer to the explanation of modern physics than the view of the modern day fundamentalist.

To illustrate how the same object can be perceived differently, the Buddha recounted an ancient parable of six blind men touching an elephant. The man who touched the head said it was a giant pot. The man who touched the tusk said it was the blade of a plow. The man who touched the trunk said it was a plow shaft. The man who touched the ear said it was a winnowing basket. The man who touched the leg said it was a pillar. The man who touched the tail said it was a brush. Similarly, each of us views the same objects from the perspective of our cultural conditioning, our life-experience, our personal aesthetics, and our intellectual capacity.

I have often been amazed by how two or more people can look at the same object and see it in totally different ways. Judging by their descriptions and reactions, you'd think they were all looking at different things. For example, a tall and very thin female model might look very attractive to one person, but sickly and anorexic to another. Some men would feel sexual attraction, while others would merely suggest she buy herself a good dinner. Some women would feel envy, and others pity. A red sunrise evokes spiritual beauty to some, but fear of impending bad weather to others. A huge diamond ring evokes intense desire in some, and worry of being robbed in others. Both the nature of the object and our emotional response to it changes from person to person.

The Buddha observed that the reality of our objects of perception is subject to interpretation. Therefore, what is real is conditioned by many factors. In a similar vein, the physicist Werner Heisenberg opined that the object we observe is not the thing in and of itself, but its appearance conditioned by the method and perspective of our inquiry. That which we perceive is always subject to the uncertainty principle because of variations in our measurements, viewing positions, and assumptions. The philosopher Immanuel Kant proposed that objective reality is known only insofar as it conforms to the essential structure of the knowing mind. Socrates explained that the objects that appear to our senses are like shadows on the walls of a cave, and their categorical names or forms are the reality behind each perception. A quote attributed to Albert Einstein says, "Reality is merely an illusion, albeit a very persistent one."

THE FOUR SEALS

Even the physical underpinnings of the objects we perceive are subject to debate. For some philosophers and scientists, the objects of perception are only projections of our minds. Others believe that material objects are composed of an infinite regression of atoms and particles. For still others, objects are the result of energy frequencies. Even the nature of light that illuminates the objects we see is subject to debate. Is light electromagnetic radiation composed of waves, particles, quanta, photons, or a combination of some or all of these?

The Buddhist theory of reality does not attempt to fully describe the physics of phenomena. Rather, it describes how we should internally view reality from the perspective of our spiritual evolution. Knowing that every phenomena can be viewed in different ways, depending on the viewing platform of the perceiver, their approach is practically oriented toward enlightened liberation from suffering. It proscribes these major principles know as the Four Seals:

1. All causal phenomena are impermanent.
2. All phenomena are empty of existing as independent entities.
3. All beings afflicted by Karma suffer.
4. *Nirvana* is peace.

Buddhist philosophy and meditation help us to precondition our minds with the wisdom of interdependence so that we are not attached to the appearance of our objects of perception. Through the wisdom generated through meditation, we learn to couple each sensory perception with an immediate internal emptying of intellectual projections, emotional responses, and false assumptions. Meditation practice helps us to observe dispassionately each object of perception as a point-instant in time, conditioned by an interdependent matrix of interdependent causes and conditions that created the object and our perception of it.

In this way, we learn to simultaneously perceive the object as it appears to our conditioned mind, as well as the causal continuum that brought it into being. In so doing, we see both its conventional way of existing and the ultimate truth of its existence. As our meditation is more and more refined, and our subtle perceptual capacities increase, we are able to intuit the past causes and future permutations of each object that appears to our senses. This capacity to see more clearly also extends to our perceptions and understandings of other people who we seek to help. Gradually, we are able to intuit the subtle, unconscious causes of their suffering and help them eliminate and heal these causes.

THE TWO TRUTHS

This way of perceiving reality is encapsulated by the Buddhist doctrine of 'Two Truths.' These are the 'Conventional Truth' *(samvritisatya)* and the 'Ultimate Truth' *(paramartha satya)*. Conventional Truths are the objects of perception that we see in our everyday lives. They are defined according to their properties of color, size, weight, density and so on. These conventionally true objects are established as real based on empirical observation of them by unimpaired senses of sight, touch, taste, smell, and hearing. They are also deemed real based on logical proof of their existence. Conventional Truths are subject to change according to refinements in our scientific understanding of the world.

The Ultimate Truth about phenomena is that everything is 'empty' of the capacity to exist on its own, independently of other cooperating causes and conditions. To help us see this more clearly, Buddhist meditations provide techniques for perceiving this 'emptiness' of inherent, independent existence. Gradually, meditation helps us to re-condition our minds so that we can stop projecting a false reality onto the objects we perceive in every day life. Meditations on the Ultimate Truth of emptiness help us to be automatically aware of the subjective elements of any perception and to empty-out these subjective misperceptions so that we can see people and things as they are, not as we want or project them to be.

Reality, for the Buddhist, is based on a radical interdependency between the perceiver (subject) and the thing (object) that is perceived. Conventional realities are those things whose existence can be validated empirically and logically. They conform to the conventions of knowing proscribed by the prevalent science and culture. The absolute reality is simply the fact that all reality is interdependent and empty of an independent mode of existence.

The result of this contemplation of both the conventional and ultimate truth of reality is that we are no longer attached to the false appearance of things; therefore, we are able to quell our desire for them as objects that have the inherent capacity to make us happy or sad. This compassionate detachment helps us see the world more clearly and to help others remove the causes of their ignorance and suffering.

The net result of this mental re-conditioning is that we are freed from our irrational attachment to things as independent causes of either our happiness or sadness. Our ability to help others is increased because we are not stuck in the drama of each momentary emotion. Our ability to transform ourselves into a liberated, compassionate, enlightened being is enhanced because we are not stuck in old paradigms that impede our progress.

Therefore, according to Buddhism, our capacity for spiritual transformation is dependent on our wisdom regarding the true nature of reality. This wisdom is honed both through intellectual learning and direct meditative perception of emptiness, the Ultimate Truth. This wisdom is then compassionately deployed to free others from the suffering caused by their ignorance of the true nature of reality.*

---

* These definitions of conventional and ultimate truth are based on a Buddhist philosophical school called *Prasangika Madhyamaka* as articulated by Nagarjuna, Chandrakirti and Tsonkhapa.

SOUL

Do I have an independent, eternal, and permanent soul?
Am I just the physical mind and body that will die when my
body dies? Is there a real 'me' that exists behind all of my
thoughts, experiences, and perceptions? Do I have a soul that
is the observer and governor of my mind and body? Is soul the
ever-changing consciousness from one life to the next?

DEPENDING ON ONE'S PERSPECTIVE, we human beings are either blessed or cursed with curiosity about our own existence. We are blessed because we have the intellectual capacity to wonder, to deduce, to dream, to experiment and search for answers. We are cursed because finding the answer to this question can often seem impossible, and can be psychologically disorienting if not approached carefully. Therefore, when it comes to the question of how I exist, it can be helpful to study with a mature mentor from an authentic wisdom tradition.

I have looked at the question of my own existence from the perspectives of philosophy, logic, physics, epistemology, psychology and in-depth readings of spiritual texts from many different traditions. Meditation and contemplation have also been invaluable tools. They provide the laboratory for empirical observation of both the gross and subtle aspects of my consciousness. Over the years, I have found that as mind becomes calmer and clearer, our conscious awareness can focus on the inner qualities that lie hidden from the five senses and intellect. Gradually, one begins to experience the mysterious and refined qualities of one's own mental continuum.

The spiritual traditions of the world offer many techniques for deep contemplation and meditation which are the keys for unlocking these secrets of the 'soul.' In addition, many of these same traditions engage the intellect to support and describe the meditative experiences normally incomprehensible to the rational mind. Working together, the faculties of intellect, meditation, contemplation and spiritual insight propel us through the maze of self-discovery.

The Mandala Process provides a framework for this self-discovery.

MY OWN EXPERIENCE WITH THE QUESTION OF SOUL

In childhood, I had a serious asthmatic condition that was occasionally life-threatening. Consequently, I was deeply fearful of dying and going completely out of existence. One late summer night as I lay in bed fearing another asthma attack, I prayed fervently for an answer to my existential question. I asked God to tell me where I came from and what would happen to me when I died. As I lay there prayerfully in a cold sweat of fear, a mysteriously decisive voice answered my prayer with these words: "You exist in someone's dream." In someone's dream! What does that mean? At that moment, my sense of comfort and relief was replaced with yet another question, "In whose dream do I exist?" Since that time, the mystery of this question has enlivened and prodded my search for an answer.

Buddhism often describes the world of our perceptions in terms of a dream-like illusion. In fact, the perception we have of our own self as an independent, permanent being, is just such an illusion. This word 'I' that we use constantly, doesn't exist as separate from the interrelated mental and physical elements of our being. Our normal sense of an independent 'I' is simply a case of mistaken identity. The 'I' is just an imaginary projection that sums up all the impermanent and interdependent elements of our existence.

The Dalai Lama explained this to me during our first private session together in 1970, which I mentioned in the Introduction:

> Where is the real Ed? Is he in your head, your chest, your stomach, your arms, or your legs? Is he all of these things? What happens if you loose a limb or an organ? Is part of Ed taken away? Or is Ed separate and aloof from all these parts of your body? Is he forever unchanging, independent of the causal changes in the body? Is he the controller of the body? But, if he is separate and immune to cause and effect, how can he interact with and have power over the body? You

see, this notion of an independent, permanent self just does not make sense. That idea of a permanent separate Ed is an illusion. The answer to your existence is much more subtle than that.

Then, in answer to my question about how I exist, he began my first lessons on the Twelve Links of Dependent Origination, which describes how it is that we are constantly born and reborn in this unsatisfactory condition called *Samsara*. Ours is a condition where each moment of happiness is inextricably linked with the causes of counter-balancing unhappiness. It is a condition wherein our attachment to the things that temporarily make us happy is also the cause our future misery—like the death of a loved one, or the burning of our home, or loss of our favorite ring. The challenge, the Dalai Lama explained, is to be compassionately engaged for the welfare of others without being attached to them as the cause of our happiness. Happiness, he explained, cannot arise solely from our relationships with others or our ownership of things. It can only arise internally from a peaceful, compassionate and wise state of mind.

TWELVE LINKS OF DEPENDENT ORIGINATION

From the Buddhist perspective, the root cause of our unsatisfactory lives is: (1) ignorance *(avidya)* about the true nature of 'I' that produces our attachment to that illusion of 'I.' This 'I' they say, doesn't exist, either as the same or different from all other interdependent elements of our being. Attachment to the notion of a permanent 'I' is the source of suffering. This way of thinking about ourselves and others gives rise to a whole series of (2) mental predispositions *(samskaras)* that are played-out in each of the following 10 Links of Dependent Origination. These mental predispositions condition the quality of our (3) conscious awareness *(vijnana)*. The quality of our consciousness gives rise to our (4) name and form *(namarupa)* of our physical body that contains the (5) six sense organs *(satayatana)* through which we perceive the external world via our eyes, ears, nose, tongue, touch and mind. It is through these senses that we make (6) contact *(phassa)* with the external world and then experience (7) sensations *(vedana)* that cause us to (8) crave *(tanha)* the objects we perceive, since they appear to existence as independent causes of happiness. Our craving intensifies in the form of (9) grasping or clinging *(upadana)* to those things and lifestyles that we think will make us happy. It is the quality of this clinging that predicts the type of (10) existence *(bhava)* we will experience in the future, whether in this life or future lives. All of these links of dependent origination condition the quality of our cycle of life from (11) birth *(jati)* to (12) old age and death *(jaramarana)*.

Now, on the surface, these might just seem like words. But when we contemplate each one, we begin to see the cause and effect in our own lives. For example, if we begin by focusing on something that we crave, we can analytically dissect the reasons for this intense desire. Working backwards, we can see that the 'craving' arose because of a pleasant 'sensation' that was caused by 'contact' through one of our 'senses,' that was caused by our particular kind of 'body' that was formed by the nature of our 'consciousness' that was preconditioned by the 'mental predispositions' that were inflicted by our 'ignorance' about the true nature of reality.

In this way, we can see how craving will become the source of our future misery, tracing back the reasons to which you were attached in the first place. What were the associated sensations from contact? How did you perceive this through your senses? What made you think it was attractive in and of itself? Was it your own ignorant misperceptions that caused you to think it was attractive, and that compelled you to grasp onto it?

This contemplative process helps us to loosen the powers of attraction and attachment, and to re-orient ourselves around higher values of wisdom and compassion. By meditating on the interdependent causes and conditions of life, we begin to alter our thought patterns and our behavior. We realize that each momentary word, thought and action is the cause of our future state of being. We begin to live more mindfully and to diminish those ways of being that lead to craving and future states of unhappiness.

From the Buddhist perspective, the 'self' or 'soul' is not a solitary, isolated, independent witness and controller of your being. Rather, it is simply a verbal designation given to the interdependent, intertwined and relational functions of our body and consciousness. While we are prone to use the words 'I' and 'myself,' this doesn't mean that there is a static and unchangeable thing to which these words refer.

When we think of our self as a separate entity, this sets up a false dichotomy and duality between the inner and outer world. It compels us to protect ourselves first and others second, to think of our own health before we consider the well-being of others. But if we see our existence as inherently relational, then we realize that our well-being is dependent on our intention for the well-being of others. Therefore, when we act in service to others, we are in fact serving ourselves.

By meditating on the interdependence of our being and compassion to alleviate the suffering of others, our own consciousness becomes purified, and our future happiness in this and subsequent lives is made possible.

So while belief in the independent, permanent soul provides solace to many, Buddhism teaches that this belief in the soul is the very cause of our suffering. Instead, it offers us this explanation: our eternal existence is rather like an ever-changing river that never runs dry.

Now you might be asking me: "How do you answer the existential question of your childhood?" How do you make sense of that mysterious voice that answered your prayer saying: "You exist in someone's dream."

Indeed, in whose dream do I exist?

Perhaps my own.

SPIRIT-BEINGS

Are there other intelligent, non-corporeal beings with whom
we communicate? Are some spirit-beings the messengers or
intermediaries with God or other divine entities? Do they have
special powers to help or guide us? Can we become such beings?
Can we rely on the messages of spirit-beings as being infallibly
true? Are spirit-beings subjective projections of our own mind?

SPIRITUAL TRADITIONS throughout the world speak with certainty
about the existence of spirit-beings. Scriptures and oral traditions
tell us about angels, archangels, devils, fairies, goddesses, dakinis,
spirit-guides, protectors, fairies, sprites and ghosts.

Eyewitness accounts of spirit-beings come from a wide variety
of people in all the world's cultures, so it is hard to completely
discount the possibility of their existence. People who have these
experiences seem to have little trouble believing in multiple worlds
and life after death.

Many spiritual traditions teach methods for contacting spirit-
beings. Often, these methods are held in secret by priests or
shamans and taught only to those whose minds are receptive,
whose faith is strong, and who are free from psychological
difficulties. For the shamanic trances and communications with
spirit-beings can often be mentally destabilizing.

The Mandala Process provides a context for examining
the question of spirit-beings from a wide variety of spiritual
perspectives.

MY OWN EXPERIENCE WITH THE QUESTION OF SPIRIT-BEINGS

In 1981, the spirit-beings of Tibet descended on the lush, rolling
farmlands of Wisconsin. Their arrival was preceded by ten years
of careful planning by Geshe Lhundup Sopa, who was among
the first Tibetan Lamas to come to America and teach at a major

university. With the help of some loyal supporters, he purchased a home about ten miles outside of Madison to become a new monastery. He then invited the Dalai Lama to come and consecrate the monastery, as well as a new temple built for the performance of an elaborate initiation into a major tantric practice called the Kalachakra.

Nowadays, visits by the Dalai Lama to the United States have become regular events. In 1989, he received the Noble Peace Prize, and since then has authored numerous books and presented public talks and religious ceremonies throughout the world. But in 1981, few people had heard of Tibetan Buddhism, or the Dalai Lama, and the exotic Buddhist initiation called the Kalachakra or 'Wheel of Time.'

Before his arrival in Wisconsin, a group of monks carried-out extensive prayers and rituals to summon the appropriate spiritual deities to the land on which the initiation would be performed. Then, about a week before the actual ceremony, the Dalai Lama arrived to join the monks in these preparations. My job, at the time, was to document the whole affair with 16mm film and video, including interviews with His Holiness about Tibetan Buddhism and this particular tantric initiation.

Until this point in time, Buddhism had been known in America primarily for its practices of meditation, its philosophy of impermanence and interdependence, and its compassionate, non-violent approach to solving life's problems. All these made good sense to early Buddhist converts, and to the general public. But the introduction of spirit-beings and tantric practices involving the transformation of emotional, kinesthetic, and somatic energy into compassionate enlightenment were beyond the imaginary possibilities of most people. Even the Tibetan lamas feared that these beliefs would be misunderstood by people in America and used to discredit the whole religion and culture. Moreover, since these practices are so powerful psychologically, they felt that initiates needed to be very carefully prepared and trained in advance. Therefore, they had traditionally kept many of these practices secret and were very careful about who they initiated into them.

In my interviews with the Dalai Lama, I asked him about these spiritual deities and how, in light of all the other more rationale aspects of Buddhism, people should understand their arrival in

America. "It is very simple," he said. "When the Indian monks brought Buddhism to Tibet, they brought their deities with them. Now, we Tibetans are bringing them to America." At the time, I was surprised by this remarkably straight-forward answer from a man who obviously had an extraordinary intellect and knew that the idea of deities might seem odd to many Americans, including myself.

From the Buddhist perspective, a deity is a being who has been transformed into a refined physical appearance that reflects their divine spiritual qualities. They are loving, compassionate and wise beings who have supernatural capacities to heal, teach and protect those human beings with whom a relationship has been established through meditation, ritual, prayer, and good *karma*. They might also be the emanations of a Buddha who has created them in order to help others. Often, a deity, like a Kalachakra deity, is associated with a particular Buddha, place or type of spiritual teaching. Exactly how these deities exist is subject to debate and interpretation. For some, they are very real beings. For others, they are imaginary, anthropomorphic representations of divine and sacred qualities of being. In either case, meditation on these iconic images of deities can provide a powerful psychological tool for actualizing the divine qualities that are the potential of every being.

Over the years, I have come to view the possibility, perhaps even the probability, of spirit-beings in the following way. We live in an infinite universe, so there are infinite possibilities for a marvelous variety of life forms. Therefore, it is possible to imagine the existence of life-forms that are very different from those generally known on earth. From a Buddhist perspective, all the living beings that occupy the three realms of the universe share common properties, including consciousness and *karma*. Even deities (unless they are projections of an enlightened Buddha) carry the *karma* of previous lives as they transmigrate from one incarnation to the next. And with each new birth, they manifest into a physical form that reflects the relative good and bad *karma* from previous lives. If they are born with the very subtle and refined body of a deity, it is because they had extremely good *karma* and have developed a very profound and refined practice of meditation.

After their death, those beings who have engaged in meditations and transformative practice in the highest degree are reborn as sublime spirit-beings whose refined physical form reflects the level of their spiritual realization. As spirit-beings, their bodies and minds have vastly greater knowledge and power than do humans. Among all the various kinds of deities, there are those who are especially associated with the Kalachakra initiation I referred to earlier. Therefore, it is these deities that are invoked and invited into the place where an initiation is held. Their job is to provide a protected environment for the initiates who will be opening their minds and hearts to a new way of perceiving reality and their human potential. These deities 'hold the space' so that the new initiates themselves can become deified, thereby embodying the qualities of wisdom and compassion on their own paths to enlightenment and liberation.

The belief in spirit-beings comes naturally and effortlessly to many indigenous peoples, whose minds have not been subjugated by the materialist dogma of modern western science. The existence of spirit-beings can be perceived in the trees, the streams, the mountains, the skies, and the land. Just because they can't be perceived through our ordinary sense organs does not mean that they don't exist. There are other, more subtle ways of knowing than through our five senses, which are only capable of detecting certain spectrums of light, frequencies of sound, vibrations of energy, textures of touch, flavors of taste, and aromas of scent.

Our senses are limited by the cellular and neurological biology of our human bodies. While other animal species can hear, see, smell, and feel far more than we, our human experience is restricted to a narrow range of energy spectra and resonance. Therefore, we have to rely on scientific instruments, mathematical calculations, and logical thinking to deduce and prove the existence of the things that lie beyond our senses. Our skepticism about the existence of other life-forms has shut down our potential for knowing and experiencing the marvelous invisible world within and around us. Our narrow minds cause us to suffer from doubt, skepticism, and even disdain for those who claim to have seen beyond the veil imposed by our feeble sensory apparatus. The fullness of our potential life-experience is often quashed by cynical disbelief.

My own personal experiences in the natural world and my sightings of ghostly beings have provided me with an experiential (empirical) foundation for my belief in the existence of spirit-beings. Therefore, in spite of the derisive comments of my peers,

I am confident in their existence. Indeed, after the completion of the Dalai Lama's ceremony in Wisconsin, a sudden wind swept through the grounds and flocks of a species of birds that no one had ever seen before circled in unison overhead. I witnessed a similar phenomena in a Buddhist monastery in Ladakh where, at the completion of a major winter ceremony, when all the malevolent energies had been dispersed, snow began falling from a sky that moments before had been perfectly clear and blue. This phenomenon had been predicted in advance as a sign of a successful ritual.

Rampant mining, industrialization, pollution, and assembly-line systems of education are all symptoms of over-reliance on the limited rational-thinking mind. Our disconnect from nature and her spirit-beings has caused us to destroy the environment to achieve short-term materialistic goals. Our modern economic, political, agricultural, and education systems have been predicated on the notion that humans are endowed with the right to exploit the earth's natural resources for the production of material products to make our lives easier and happier. We have been deluded into thinking that happiness and well-being can result from the things we produce from nature, rather than by enjoying the exquisite beauty of the natural world itself.

We have systematically exterminated our innate relationship with the spirits of nature and the sacredness of the natural world. One of the reasons we have done this is because our belief in the deities of nature would prevent us from destroying the lands in which they live. I believe that if we had continued to believe in the sacredness of nature and the spirit-beings that reside within, the moral compass of our civilization would have prevented us from going down the path of destroying the natural world.

I have found that the ancient Buddhist and other indigenous perspectives can help us to rediscover a state of interdependence, kinship and well-being that emerge from our relationship with the natural world. These perspectives can help us to recover our sense of the sacred, and of the existence of spirit-beings in the environment around us. These perspectives can help us to expand our sense of self beyond the narrow confines of an isolated permanent soul locked in the skin of our bodies, and to experience a dynamic sense of self that is intertwined in reciprocal relationship with all beings, seen and unseen, throughout the universe.

These perspectives can be found in all the spiritual traditions of the world, and in the hearts of people in all religions. It is in this re-connection with each other and the spirit-beings of nature that we have the opportunity to heal ourselves and the earth.

SUFFERING

What is suffering? What is the cause of suffering?
Can we eliminate suffering? What is the cure for suffering?

EACH OF US WILL EXPERIENCE some form of physical pain, whether it be from injury, sickness, disease, fatigue or hunger. And we will also experience some form of emotional pain whether it be from loneliness, rejection, stress, poverty, unfulfilled desires, injustice or the death of someone we love. For most of us, pain begets suffering.

By suffering, I mean both the obvious emotions, such as anguish, misery, agony, torment, as well as the subtle emotions like stress, worry and dissatisfaction. Looking for the cause of our misery, we often blame society, the government, our parents, germs, violent entertainment, fatty foods, pollution, or dangerous toys. We cry out to God, "Why are you doing this to me?!" We bemoan our 'fate' as if there is nothing we can do to avoid the periodic agonies of human existence.

Sometimes we blame ourselves, our lifestyles, our poor decisions, our selfishness, greed or stupidity for our suffering. If we aren't careful, taking personal responsibility can deteriorate into a self-blame and self-hate that results in even more personal suffering and destructive behavior. The trick is to find the key to unlock the inner secrets of suffering that ennoble our human dignity and capacity without eroding our confidence that we can transform the causes of suffering into the causes of happiness.

For the Buddhist monks with whom I have studied, the Truth of Suffering is the starting-place for spiritual practice. Suffering is regarded as the consequence of ignorance about the true nature of reality and of seeking happiness in all the wrong places. The Buddhist Path is designed to free those who follow it from suffering and its causes.

Transforming and healing the causes of suffering is the root-calling of spiritual inquiry, insight and practice. In my life, I have worked with some extraordinary people who have done just this, and I'd like to give you a little sample of my own experience with the question of suffering.

MY OWN EXPERIENCE WITH THE QUESTION OF SUFFERING

In the 1970s, I lived and worked among the Tibetan refugees who had escaped the brutal cultural genocide at the hands of the Chinese army that invaded their country. They endured unimaginable hardships during their escape over the snowy passes of the high Himalayas only to find themselves in abject poverty in the northern plains of India. Some of these refugees were highly revered Tibetan Buddhist monks and nuns, now penniless, yet determined to preserve the ancient traditions of Buddhism that originally came to Tibet from India, the land in which they now sought refuge. A few of these monks became my teachers, and I studied with them in the poor refugee monasteries in India.

One of these monks was an esteemed teacher (later abbot of Sera Che Monastery) named Geshe Lobsang Donyo, who I first met him in Bodhgaya in March of 1978. I had traveled there with Geshe Lhundup Sopa who had been one of the first Tibetan monks to come to America and teach at a major university. He was both my spiritual teacher and my major professor for my doctoral studies at the University of Wisconsin-Madison. We, along with thousands of other monks and Tibetan refugees, were in Bodhgaya to receive teachings from His Holiness the Dalai Lama, who sat under a tree that marked the exact place where the Buddha was said to have become enlightened 2,500 years earlier.

Geshe Donyo had survived his first refugee years in India working on a road crew comprised of hundreds refugees employed to crush rocks with a hammer. His only possessions were his robes, a few tattered books, a beaded rosary, a portable stove, a cooking pot, a bowl and a spoon. Yet he was the most good-natured, cheerful person I had ever met. Observing him, I noticed how his lips were constantly shaping the prayers and mantras that he said internally, and his soft eyes always betrayed the quiescence of his meditative mind that rested in the background of everything he did.

Together, we spent a good deal of time circumambulating the central temple and the Bodhi Tree, and in conversations about

Buddhism and his experience as a refugee in India. Whenever we separated and I said in Tibetan, "See you later," he replied with a smile, "If I don't die first!" I gradually learned how Geshe Donyo's spiritual practice had kept his mind peaceful and loving during the travails of refugee life, and how he was constantly prepared for death whenever it would come.

A short time later, I stayed with Geshe Donyo in his small room at his refugee Tantric monastery called Gyudmed in Southern India, where he taught the esoteric practices he had learned from the lineage of his Tibetan teachers that traced back to India over a thousand years ago. Gyudmed was very poor, with just a trickle of electricity in a few bulbs, very little fresh water, and primitive sanitation facilities. Here the monks continued their study and practice while building a new monastery with barely enough food to keep them going. I slept on the dirt floor of Geshe Donyo's room and shared simple meals of rice and vegetables cooked on his tiny stove and cooking pot.

I learned how his internal practice had harnessed all the mental attributes that I have come to call 'archetypal spiritual styles.' On his wall was a ragged painting of a Tantric image of the Buddha that he clearly imagined in his own mind (an example of the Way of Arts and Imagination). His physical practices included prostrations, mudras (hand gestures), ritual dance, walking meditation, and work (all examples of the Way of the Body). His mind was in a continual state of meditation on the emptiness and interdependence of all phenomena (i.e, the Way of Contemplation and Meditation). His meditatively refined intuition enabled him to perceive the inner causes of suffering in others, and to commune with spirit-beings to help those who came to him for guidance (i.e., the Way of the Mystic.) His interactions and perceptions of the unseen forces and beings in the environment gave him wisdom beyond our normal capacities (i.e., participating in the Way of Nature). His internal prayers and rituals were a constant grounding for his practice (i.e., the Way of Prayer). He had achieved the highest degrees of intellectual learning in his tradition, which provided him with a rational foundation for his spiritual practices and teachings (i.e., the Way of Reason). He was constantly teaching and helping others to expand and deepen their practice of Buddhism (i.e., participating in the Way of Relationships). He had achieved a profound, direct, non-conceptual knowledge of the true nature of existence (an outcome of the Way of Wisdom).

It was through Geshe Donyo and other teachers like Father Thomas Keating, Rabbi Zalman Schachter-Shalomi, Swami Atmarupananda, and the Dalai Lama, that I witnessed fully mature spiritual beings whose practices harnessed all the twelve archetypal spiritual styles and answered all twelve universal spiritual questions. Each of these Buddhist and non-Buddhist teachers exemplified how suffering is cured by wisdom and unconditional compassion. These two qualities, wisdom and compassion, are like the two wings of a bird that flies to freedom from the cage of *Samsara,* the world of suffering.

(I have written about wisdom and compassion elsewhere, so I won't say more here; but I have described one of my successful experiments in healing the suffering of chronic back pain in the appendix of this book.)

TRANSFORMATION
& ULTIMATE POTENTIAL

What is the highest potential for my existence?
Do I have the potential to transform myself into my
ideal being? Is it possible to become a Christ, Buddha, Moses, or
an enlightened being? Is my natural state-of-being pure
and enlightened? How should I engage in my own
transformative process?

JUST AS THE CATERPILLAR is transformed into the butterfly, we are in a continual process of transformation, moving through the stages of infancy, childhood, adolescence, adulthood, middle age, old age, and death. Within these stages of life, we are in a constant process of change; so much so, that we might not even recognize ourselves at a previous stage of our life. But, since we generally retain our birth name and our social security number, we often fall for the illusion that we are the exact same person throughout the different stages of our lives.

Change and transformation are the hallmarks of life. But are we evolving? Can we honestly chart a qualitative change in our development as we move through the stages of life? How often have we stepped off life's treadmill to take an honest look at our lives, made goals for improvements, and charted strategies for becoming the person we would really like to be?

Growing up in the First Presbyterian Church in Cedar Rapids, Iowa, no one ever suggested that the goal of a good Christian was to actually become Jesus. It would have been considered delusional to have such an ambition! People have been scoffed at for far less ambitious visions. And yet, that is what many of the world's great spiritual traditions propose that we should do.

The Mandala Process encourages us to begin with our 'big questions' and the recognition of our personal spiritual styles, our personal archetypes for transformation. Each of us begins where we are now, exploring our unique combination of spiritual styles, questions, experiences and karmic propensities. We begin our search for answers, for teachers and practices that are right for us. At some point along our paths, we seek the guidance of authentic, experienced mentors who have already traveled a long way on the journey and can share the fruits of their own experiences. While many principles and practices are similar among the paths, we will still need authentic guides from within a tradition to help us harness our archetypal spiritual styles so that we can sort through the nuances and avoid the pitfalls along the way.

Just as when we recognize that we are sick and seek medical treatment from a good doctor, we begin the transformative journey with an objective analysis of our present life-situation; we envision the ideal toward which we are striving; we assess the internal predispositions and capabilities we will activate; we choose the best 'maps' for leading us to our destination; and then we seek training for the journey.

Perhaps our most important challenge is to perform an honest assessment of the combined qualities of our mind, body and spirit, and evaluate the extent to which these are integrated and moving forward in harmony towards a state of being we truly want and respect. The Spiritual Styles and Questions Profile Tools help us get started on this process

Buddhist teachers often compare our present condition to a prison in which we are confined by the limits of our imagination, shackled by our ignorance, bound by our senses, hamstrung by of our desire, attachment and anger, constricted by our intellectual doubt and weakened by our lack of will-power for self-liberation. Even if we are provided with a plan for escape, few of us actually have the trust, confidence, willpower, and stamina to free ourselves. Most of us simply remain in prison, absorbed by the small pleasures of life, anesthetized by alcohol, drugs, sensual distractions, and deluded by false promises of happiness through things and relationships. We are afraid to peek outside the walls of our safe little worlds to be inspired by the infinite possibilities of being. We avoid the possibility that we could be internally free and help others to escape the same prison walls.

Great teachers from many traditions tell us that the journey to freedom cannot start with selfish intentions. It begins with the vow to help others to be free. But doing so requires us to make the journey for ourselves so that we can return to show others the way. That is the example set by such archetypal saviours as Moses, Jesus, Mohammed, Lao Tsu, Ramakrishnan, and Black Elk. In Mahayana Buddhism, this is called the path of the Bodhisattva, the one whose compassion for others spurs them on to enlightenment. Then, free of their own internal shackles, they show others how to loosen the chains of their own delusion and attachment so that they might in turn help others to be free.

The Spiritual Paths Mandala helps us to explore teachings on transformation from many different traditions and to find the ones that match our spiritual styles and helps answer our questions.

My Experience with the Question of Transformation

Amidst the marvelous diversity of the world's spiritual traditions, the following statement might be acceptable:

All spiritual traditions believe that transformation toward a wise and loving state-of-being is possible.

Assuming this statement is true, we can only marvel at the extraordinary diversity of methods for this transformation with all the world's religious and spiritual traditions. What a marvelous tapestry of spiritual maps, methods and destinations we humans have created!

If we look within each specific religion, we find a remarkable diversity of transformative goals and methods. Then, if we broaden our gaze to compare and contrast this diversity among all the traditions, we discover that each of these diverse approaches has its counter-part within all of the other traditions. These similarities are reflections of the shared spiritual archetypal styles among the adherents of each faith tradition. The processes and practices are similar because of the archetypal similarities among their authors and practitioners.

We can see these similarities, for example, if we compare the poetic language of Christian, Islamic, Jewish, and Hindu mystics. If you leave off the name used for God, you would think they were all from the same religion. They sound the same because they are written by people who are expressing themselves through the shared archetypal style of the Mystic.

And yet, these wonderful similarities in spiritual style cannot hide the fascinating diversity of belief regarding final goals for transformation. For example, some Christians believe the humans are born in "original sin" that can only be purified by acceptance of Jesus Christ as one's lord and savior. Their transformative goal is to be saved from hell-fire and granted a heavenly hereafter. Theirs is a dualistic practice in which the individual soul will always remain separate yet blessed by the grace of God. On the other hand, there are some Hindus who believe that the transformative goal is to consciously re-unite their individual soul *(atman)* in non-dual union with the divine creator *(Brahman)* through prayers, chants, rituals, and meditation. There are native peoples who believe the Earth and all its animals, plants, and minerals are sacred. Their goal is to merge our individual identity with that of the divine energy of nature. There are Muslims who believe that humans are the creation of Allah and the transformative goal of religious practice is to be granted an eternal existence in a heavenly paradise once this human life has ended.

Even among Buddhists, there exist a diversity of sects and transformative goals. For some Theravada Buddhists, the goal is to achieve *nirvana* which is a transcendent state of eternal bliss. Pure Land Buddhists hope to be reborn in a heaven presided over by a Buddha where they can continue their journey to enlightenment.

For some Mahayana Buddhists, the transformative goal is to actually become a Buddha. This is possible, they say, because we all have 'Buddha Nature,' i.e., the innate potential to become a perfectly compassionate, all-knowing being. Therefore, the goal of spiritual practice is to awaken this Buddha Nature within us through a combination of ethical conduct, prayer, ritual, mantra, visualization and meditation. This Buddhist transformative process is designed to help each individual to actualize their inner Buddha Nature.

The transformative goals of religions are so profound that they require us to harness and harmonize all the spiritual styles within us in order to achieve them. In Buddhism, for example, we might begin by visualizing the goal of Buddhahood as it is depicted by various artistic statues and paintings. These images depict the benevolent compassion, fierce wisdom, healing power, and meditative quiescence of the Buddha.

Inspired by these images, the Buddhist practitioner will create a loving and compassionate intention to become liberated and enlightened for the sole purpose of helping others to be free from suffering. This intention is stated in the Bodhisattva Vow, which is the actual entry-point into Mahayana Buddhist practice. The intention is beautifully stated in the following verse:

> And now, as long as space endures,
> As long as there are beings to be found,
> May I continue likewise to remain,
> To drive away the sorrows of the world.*

Because the process of transformation from our normal human self into that of a Buddha is so difficult, Buddhist practitioners engage in an extensive combination of prayers, mantras, intellectual learning, and meditations to propel them along their journeys. Implicitly, the specific combination of transformative processes might vary according to the predominate spiritual styles of each practitioner. Depending on one's style, a person might focus on painting and sculpture, music, prayer, ritual, reason, meditation, or physical work. Then, over the course of a lifetime, one's style might shift, as gradually the different aspects of one's personality become engaged in the transformative process. In this way, a person gradually brings all aspects of their being into the practice of transformation.

Among the mature teachers with whom I have worked over the years, I have found that they have engaged all these archetypal spiritual styles around the same transformative goals and purposes.

For me, the transformative process began with the questions: Who am I? And why am I here? These questions led me to the study and practice of Buddhism where I could fully engage the full spectrum of my mind, body and spirit. What began with an intellectual inquiry and a few seemingly mystical experiences, led into the practice of meditation where I could begin cultivating mental calm and focused insight into the nature of reality. This meditation helped to reveal, heal, and empty the unconscious conceptual and emotional obstacles, allowing my natural capacity for wisdom and compassion to arise and infuse all aspects of my being.

Throughout my time in India, I often attended elaborate Tibetan

---

* Shantideva, *Way of the Bodhisattva*, 10:55.

Buddhist rituals and received initiations into Buddhist Tantras. But at the time, these types of practices did not resonate with my primary styles of intellectual reason and meditation because they seemed to entail faith and devotion to supernatural beings that were imaginary and not empirically knowable. Nevertheless, I tried to keep an open mind and find a reason to engage in these practices. Then, gradually over the course of many years, all of my archetypal spiritual styles, even the Way of Imagination, became engaged in the process of transformation. Gradually, the process of emptying the false sense of self, and surrender to a grander possibility of being, became a natural form of spiritual practice and expression.

The Buddhist Tantras employ the full spectrum of spiritual practice in order to propel transformation. Tantric practitioners imagine and visualize the ideal being (i.e., deity) that they would like to become, and then set out to transform themselves into that being in this lifetime. Colorful paintings *(thangkas)* provide visual images of Buddhas and Bodhisattvas for focusing their attention and intention. Geometrically designed mandalas provide a visual representation of a sacred space to 'enter into' for spiritual practice. Verbal mantras stimulate and awaken powerful mental capacities and bring their voice into play. Prayers invoke the presence and the help of deities. Hand gestures *(mudra)* and dance-like movements enable their body to emulate the body of the deity. Internal breath control withdraws consciousness from the normal organs of sense, and focuses it on the vital energy in the heart center *(chakra)* of the body. Focused imagination and transmutation of psychic and physical energies from their heart-centers transform their normal energetic states of being into the divine qualities and powers of the imagined deity. Finally, the practitioner actually becomes the deity and fully actualizes the wisdom, compassion and power to help others. The ultimate transformative goal, then, is for them to become the Buddha.

Proponents and practitioners of the Buddhist Tantras believe that these practices speed up the process of transformation. It fascinates me that these practices engage all our archetypal spiritual styles—bringing all aspects of our conceptual, imaginal, physical, sensual, psychic, and emotional being into the process of transformation.

For me, this is a grand experiment in the discovery and

actualization our full human potential. It is up to each one of us to discern the goal, purpose, and process of transformation that best suits our spiritual style and temperament. Buddhism, as with all of the world's spiritual traditions, provides a diverse and profound variety of practices to help us achieve our respective goals. The grand adventure is in the exploration, discovery and the transformation that actually unfolds.

May you be transformed into the grandest ideal being that you can imagine!

PART III
YOUR SPIRITUAL PROFILE

THE MANDALA ITSELF does not provide any answers; it merely facilitates a process of discovery. It is a tool an individual can use to find a personal path, to find answers to personal questions and appropriate practices that can lead to spiritual transformation. Thus, I have included here Spiritual Profiling Tools to help you discern your predominate spiritual styles and your major questions.

The ranking of your spiritual styles is not fixed or final. It is merely a snapshot of the prominence of these styles at this time in your life. The main purpose of this instrument is to help you look within, beneath the surface of your mind, to explore and discover the styles that subconsciously influence your spiritual predispositions and choices. Once you are aware of these, you can begin to harness them in the service of your personal spiritual development. While this Mandala identifies twelve families of styles, you might uncover and then harness a style that is not included here. This is good! The purpose is to stimulate the process of discovery, not to be limited by a new dogma.

THE SPIRITUAL STYLES
PROFILING TOOL™

THIS INSTRUMENT WILL HELP YOU identify your own spiritual styles, or at least those which are predominate at this stage of your life.

STEP 1: RANKING YOUR SPIRITUAL PREFERENCES

Read the following questions and give yourself a numerical rating indicating your level of resonance with these statements.

> 1=Strongly Disagree
> 2=Mostly Disagree
> 3=Neutral
> 4=Mostly Agree
> 5=Strongly Agree

1. I am naturally comfortable with creative or artistic expression.
2. I naturally feel emotional states in my physical body.
3. I like to observe the inner workings of my mind silently and without distraction.
4. I naturally tend to be devoted to jobs, people, ideologies, or communities.
5. I often have vivid and memorable dreams.
6. I am naturally kind-hearted in my feelings toward others.
7. I am attracted to the possibility of mystical visions and revelations.
8. I find tranquility in forests, mountains, deserts, streams, lakes, or oceans.

9. I am inclined to pray to God, a higher power, or to the universal consciousness.
10. I like to ponder the universal questions of existence.
11. I am naturally inclined to close relationships with family, friends, and colleagues.
12. I believe it is possible to gain wisdom from a source beyond the senses and intellect.
13. I am inspired by artistic expressions of a spiritual nature.
14. I gravitate toward a specific physical activity to foster peace, tranquility, and insight.
15. I am comfortable spending considerable time alone.
16. I am more prone to faith than skepticism.
17. I am drawn to spiritual symbols, icons, and imagery.
18. My primary life-intention is to help others achieve their highest ideals.
19. I have had paranormal experiences.
20. I feel that nature is my connection with the sacred.
21. I have a daily ritual prayer for help, guidance, or protection from a higher power.
22. I like to thoroughly consider something before committing myself to it.
23. I gain profound insights about the nature of life through relationships with others.
24. I yearn for wisdom of the true nature of reality.
25. I gain insight and equanimity from looking at and listening to artistic works.
26. I need a physical practice that fosters peace, spiritual presence and insight.
27. I like to carefully consider all the angles before committing to a course of action.
28. I feel that a devotional practice will enhance my spiritual transformation.
29. I naturally form an image or a vision of my future goals.
30. I am naturally motivated to help remove suffering in others.

31. I have had unexplainable experiences of the supernatural.

32. I feel oneness or interbeing when immersed in the natural world.

33. I feel that prayer is an essential part of spiritual practice.

34. I prefer reason over faith.

35. I like to help others to learn, to solve problems, make decisions, and become happy.

36. I long for an enlightened wisdom in order to help others.

37. I am comfortable observing and creating art relating to my spirituality.

38. I prefer physical movement as a vehicle for spiritual/ contemplative practice.

39. I am called to discover truth through inner contemplation and meditation.

40. I believe that devotion to a sacred/higher power is required for spiritual realization.

41. I am naturally interested in mythological stories and archetypal beings.

42. I have natural empathy and feel moved to help others who are suffering.

43. I feel connection to an unnamable higher being, or universal power.

44. I feel a special spiritual affinity with certain animals or plants.

45. I believe there are supra-human beings that can hear my prayers and help me.

46. I am inclined to ask the big 'Why?' rather than regular 'how' questions.

47. I think that spiritual practice requires love, kindness, and compassion toward others.

48. I believe that some beings have attained transcendent wisdom of ultimate reality.

49. I am inspired to express my deepest feelings through music, dance, art, or poetry.

50. I naturally want to physically express my innermost insights through movement.

51. I wish to emulate those who achieve realization through meditative solitude.

52. I yearn to be devoted to a greater cause or higher principle.

53. I have had a rich and vivid imagination since childhood.

54. I feel held in a universal love and compassion from a source beyond me.

55. I am drawn to an unseen mystery that could reveal the ultimate nature of reality.

56. I regard nature as my church, spiritual source, or religion.

57. I receive a special peace and tranquility when I pray.

58. I regard reason as a necessary foundation for a spiritual practice.

59. I prefer being in the company of others more than solitude.

60. I have the potential to attain the wisdom of Buddha, Christ, La Tzu, Muhammad or Moses.

STEP 2: CALCULATING YOUR SPIRITUAL PREFERENCES

In the table below, please copy and then add up the numerical rankings you gave for each statement in Step 1.

1. Arts	#	Rank	2. Body	#	Rank
Creativity	1		Emotion	2	
Inspiration	13		Tendency	14	
Equanimity	25		Need	26	
Spirituality	37		Movement	38	
Feelings	49		Insights	50	
	Total			**Total**	

3. Contemplation	#	Rank	4. Devotion	#	Rank
Observation	3		Devotion	4	
Solitude	15		Faith	16	
Consideration	27		Transform	28	
Discovery	39		Realization	40	

| Realization | 51 | | Cause | 52 | |
| Total | | | Total | | |

5. Imagination	#	Rank	**6. Love**	#	Rank
Dreams	5		Kind-hearted	6	
Symbols	17		Intention	18	
Goals	29		Helping	30	
Mythic	41		Empathy	42	
Imagination	53		Compassion	54	
Total			Total		

7. Mystic	#	Rank	**8. Nature**	#	Rank
Attraction	7		Tranquility	8	
Paranormal	19		Connection	20	
Supernatural	31		Interbeing	32	
Higher Being	43		Affinity	44	
Mystery	55		Religion	56	
Total			Total		

9. Prayer	#	Rank	**10. Reason**	#	Rank
Higher Power	9		Questions	10	
Ritual	21		Considering	22	
Essential	33		Reason	34	
Beings	45		Why?	46	
Peace	57		Foundation	58	
Total			Total		

11. Relationships	#	Rank	**12. Wisdom**	#	Rank
Closeness	11		Beyond	12	
Insights	23		Reality	24	
Helping	35		Helping	36	
Compassion	47		Attainment	48	
Solitude	59		Potential	60	
Total			Total		

STEP 3: YOUR SPIRITUAL STYLES MANDALA

In the diagram below, please use pencils or markers to color in your Spiritual Styles Mandala based on your preferences.

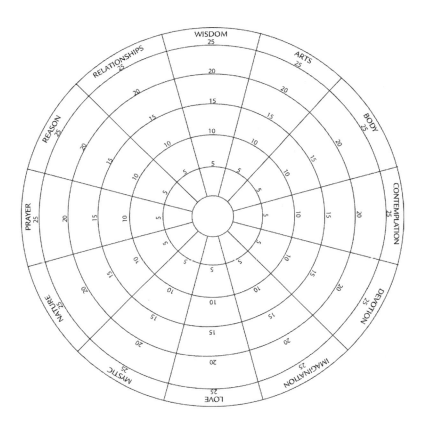

THE SPIRITUAL QUESTIONS
PROFILING TOOL™

THIS INSTRUMENT WILL HELP YOU identify your own spiritual questions, or at least those which are predominate at this stage of your life.

STEP 1: RANKING YOUR SPIRITUAL QUESTIONS
Read the following questions and rank your interest in them.

> 1= Very Uninterested
> 2= Uninterested
> 3= Neutral
> 4= Interested
> 5= Very Interested

1. What is consciousness?
2. What is death?
3. What is existence?
4. What is freedom?
5. What is God?
6. What is the meaning of 'Good'?
7. What is happiness?
8. What is reality?
9. What is the soul?
10. Do spirit-beings (angels, fairies, earth spirits, etc.) exist?
11. What is suffering?
12. What is my ultimate potential?
13. Is consciousness physical, and does it die with the body?

14. When my body dies is that the end of my existence?
15. Is there a beginning and end to existence?
16. Is true freedom possible?
17. Does God have gender and personality?
18. What is meaning and cause of evil?
19. Is happiness the same as fun and enjoyment?
20. Does the external world exist just as I perceive it?
21. Do I have a soul, and is it the real me?
22. Are there spirit-beings with whom we can communicate?
23. Why do we suffer?
24. What is my capacity to be transformed?
25. What is the potential of consciousness?
26. Is physical death just a natural event in my continued existence?
27. Did existence begin with God?
28. How can I be free?
29. Am I created in the image of God?
30. Are good and evil mutually dependent?
31. Is it possible to by happy all the time?
32. Is reality dependent on my perception of it?
33. Is my soul created by God?
34. Are there spirit-beings who are messengers of God, or benevolent helpers?
35. What is the cause of suffering?
36. How can I actualize my highest potential?
37. Is consciousness universal or particular to each being?
38. How can I die before I die and live more fully?
39. Does existence evolve, and does it have a purpose?
40. Do I have free will and freedom of choice?
41. Does God observe or control my personal life?
42. How can I be truly good?
43. How can I become forever happy?
44. How can I know the true nature of reality?

45. Is my soul permanent and eternal?

46. Can we rely on the messages of spirit-beings as infallibly true?

47. Can we eliminate suffering?

48. Does transformation require eliminating obstacles or acquiring new capacities?

49. Is consciousness the basis of my existence?

50. How can death be seen as a gift rather than a threat?

51. Does the existence of existence depend on my perception of it?

52. Can there be freedom without bondage?

53. Is God just a name for the unnamable power and mystery of existence?

54. Must I be good to be happy?

55. Is it possible to be happy while relieving the suffering of others?

56. Must I understand the true nature of reality to become happy and free?

57. Do I have a soul, or core of my being that is eternal yet ever changing?

58. Are spirit-beings just subjective projections of one's own consciousness?

59. What is the cure for suffering?

60. What practices for transformation are right for me?

STEP 2: CALCULATING YOUR SPIRITUAL PREFERENCES

In the table below, please copy and then add up the numerical rankings you gave for each statement in Step 1.

1. Consciousness	#	Rank	2. Death	#	Rank
Consciousness	1		Death	2	
Physical	13		Body	14	
Potential	25		Existence	26	
Universal	37		Living Fully	38	

| Existence | 49 | | Gift | 50 | |
| Total | | | | Total | |

3. Existence	#	Rank	4. Freedom	#	Rank
Existence	3		Freedom	4	
Beginning	15		Possibility	16	
God	27		How?	28	
Evolution	39		Free Will	40	
Perception	51		Bondage	52	
Total				Total	

5. God	#	Rank	6. Good / Evil	#	Rank
God	5		Good	6	
Personality	17		Evil	18	
Image	29		Good & Evil	30	
Control	41		Truly Good	42	
Mystery	53		Happy	54	
Total				Total	

7. Happiness	#	Rank	8. Reality	#	Rank
Happiness	7		Reality	8	
Enjoyment	19		Externality	20	
Possibility	31		Perception	32	
Forever Happy	43		True Nature	44	
Suffering	55		Understand	56	
Total				Total	

9. Soul	#	Rank	10. Beings	#	Rank
Soul	9		Spirit-beings	10	
Real Me	21		Communicate	22	
Created	33		Messengers	34	
Eternal	45		Infallibility	46	
Changing Core	57		Projections	58	
Total				Total	

11. Suffering	#	Rank	12. Trans.	#	Rank
Suffering	11		Potential	12	
Why?	23		Capacity	24	
Cause	35		Actualize	36	
Eliminate	47		Obstacles	48	
Cure	59		Practices	60	
	Total			**Total**	

STEP 3: YOUR SPIRITUAL QUESTIONS MANDALA

In the diagram below, please use pencils or markers to color in your Spiritual Questions Mandala based on your preferences.

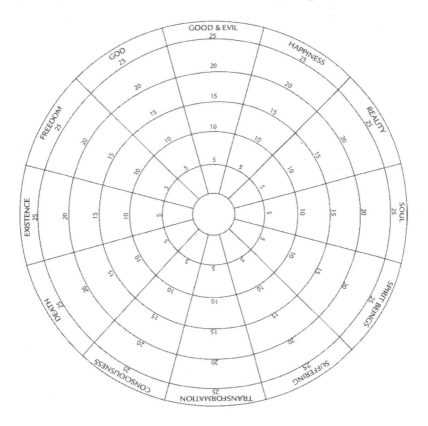

YOUR NEXT STEPS

WORK WITH THE SPIRITUAL PATHS MANDALA is further deepened through an engagement with the seven steps of InterSpiritual Meditation . This meditative and contemplative process is designed to be customized by each individual according to their own spiritual style and questions. It is a method for gaining deep insight and direct experience into the nature and purpose of our lives. Together, the Mandala Process and InterSpiritual Meditation help us to develop a solid and sustainable inner foundation for integrating and bringing our deepest insights and values into the world. For more information on these, formation on these offerings, please visit the web-site: *www.spiritualpaths.net.*

APPENDIX A
"THE MANDALA VISION"

IN MY TRAVELS IN ASIA, I wandered through many ancient landscapes and sacred temples, and saw many ancient sites. But the place where I discovered the Mandala exists only in the geography of my imagination. It is neither real nor unreal.

It is situated near the tributary of the ancient Silk Trade route that wound through Central Asia in the ancient regions of Kashgar. It lies just a few hours walk from a trading center where merchants and seekers once gathered from the diverse cultures of such regions as India, Tibet, China, Mongolia, Siberia, Southeast Asia, Persia, Mesopotamia, Assyria, Greece, Rome and Egypt. It was here that a temple was created to celebrate the marvelous diversity of ideas, arts, beliefs, and spiritual practices from all these regions of the world. The temple contained an unmatched collection of scriptures, paintings, sculptures, and religious relics.

I learned all this from my imaginal journey to the top of a hill in the center of a broad valley surrounded in the distance by tall mountains. The hill rises above verdant agricultural fields irrigated by waters from a slow flowing river. I wandered there on a warm, sunny, late-summer afternoon as fluffy white clouds provided intermittent shade and a gentle breeze blew in from the west. The top of the hill was covered by vegetation growing between rough-hewn stones—vegetation that was closely manicured by goats that wandered up to graze. On that day, there were a few goat herders resting on the fallen stones along with some men and women from a nearby village.

At first, I walked around the full perimeter of the hilltop along the row of stones that had once formed a wall about fifty meters in diameter. As I circumambulated counter-clockwise around the wall, I paused at the southernmost boundary where the wall seemed to drop off, as if it were the site of the original entrance.

And then I descended to the ground and walked directly north, zigzagging around stones that seemed to form rooms around a central courtyard. At about ten meters from the north edge of the perimeter, I stopped before a jumble of rocks that rose a meter or two. It felt as though like I was approaching an altar of an ancient temple.

As I stepped forward, I instinctively got down on my hands and knees and began to look beneath the rubble. I began lifting up some of the smaller stones to see what I might find. As I peered through the cracks between the stones, a faint circular image began to appear about a meter in diameter. It was carved into a flat stone that had been partially cracked and broken. There were three concentric circles each containing twelve geometric shapes. On a few of the shapes, there was the faint residue of color. This image appeared to be an ancient mandala that served as a sacred symbol the might have hung on the front of the altar. It seemed to have been a colored geometric design that symbolized the ideology and practices of the spiritual tradition that once resided there.

It was not possible to remove this broken stone altarpiece because of the heavy stones lying over it. The fragments were just too fragile to be moved without doing greater damage. Also, it just seemed wrong to remove anything from this site. This broken mandala seemed to belong here as a sacred relic of a profound vision and extraordinary moment in history.

As I kneeled there before the altar, an elderly man from that region approached me. He was dressed in the loose fitting garb of the region; his demeanor was friendly, and his soft piercing eyes asked for a deeper purpose for my visit. He asked: "Who are you? What brought you here?" I told him that I was drawn to this place because of my interest in the world's ancient and diverse spiritual traditions. I felt that beneath their cultural forms and rote rituals they shared a profound message about the spiritual capacities all beings. I told him that I had dreamt of this place and that I had come on a pilgrimage to this spot to fulfill my inner spiritual longing.

With that he began to tell me a story that had been passed down from parents to children over fifty generations. As he did so, a few of the other visitors and shepherds gathered around, seating themselves on the stones of the fallen alter. Although he spoke to me in broken English, the others hung on every word, for they too knew the story in their own local language.

He told me about the olden days when caravans of traders and spiritual pilgrims passed through this valley to a vibrant trading center that was just a few hours away. These caravans of camels, horses and donkeys, and people on foot could still be seen just three generations ago before the Second World War and the dominance of the communist empires of Russia and China. He remembered the excitement of this trading center, for he used to wander it as a boy with his father and grandfather whose family estate was used by traders from many lands for over a thousand years. It was on their land that merchants and pilgrims pitched their tents and traded their goods with people who came from as far away as the Mediterranean Sea to the west, the Pacific Ocean the east, and the Indian Ocean to the south. Here they would also share their music and stories, as well as their religious and spiritual traditions.

He told me how his ancestors would collect the ancient stories, beliefs and practices from priests of the many diverse religions. And, they would also collect artifacts and scriptures and preserve them in their big home. Their family wealth enabled them to support the creation of a new temple where all these objects could be stored, and where followers of many traditions could come to talk with each other, compare notes, and create a new set of practices that were inclusive of all traditions. This temple had become a pilgrimage, a way station, a refuge and a source of blessings for journeyers and seekers from many lands.

The universal spiritual inclusivity of this valley and its unique temple became a beacon of hope amidst an ancient world where religion, power, tribal affiliation, and individual salvation were tightly wrapped together. The neighboring kingdom was ruled by a monarch who claimed that his divine right of authority was granted solely to him by a single celestial god. Surrounding this divine ruler was a class of priests that presided over the rites and rituals that controlled the beliefs and behaviors of the people. The people believed that their security, peace and prosperity required unquestioned allegiance to the monarch and obedience to the priests. Any deviation from this rigid standard was punishable by banishment, imprisonment, or even death.

Therefore, this adjacent valley and temple to diverse spiritual inclusivity became a refuge for people fleeing the kingdom and it became a threat to the tyrannical rule and restrictive religious controls. As a result, the ruler and his priests became increasingly fearful that the ideology of spiritual diversity of this valley would weaken their restrictive monotheistic bond and the power and stability that was sanctified by divine rule. Therefore, with the blessing of the priests, the king ordered his army to destroy the temple along with all its precious icons, scriptures, artwork, and relics.

Today, all that remains is the rubble of a ruined temple and the faint remnants of the mandala that once symbolized its universal spiritual inclusivity. According to my guide, the mission of this temple was to celebrate the unique personalities, questions and predispositions of all the individuals who came there. Its mission was to help each individual to craft his or her own spiritual path, whether it emerges from their own native traditions, or from among the traditions represented in the temple. The temple honored spiritual diversity rather than monotheistic uniformity. He explained to me that the broken mandala beneath the ruble of the altar symbolized this vision.

With the destruction of the temple the artworks, scriptures, and inclusive practices gradually faded. Yet some of the old families of the valley still revere the right of each individual to pursue their own spiritual inclinations, so long as their path doesn't claim moral superiority over the path of another.

As we sat together, I felt as if I had come home. I felt that finally I was among true spiritual friends who could look deeply inside my heart and give credence to my own spiritual yearnings. I felt a sense of freedom and exhilaration to finally release my true aspiration to the world. I felt that the beacon of light from that ancient temple had been burning within my own heart. And I vowed to honor and to nourish the flickers of this light burning within the hearts of all beings.

This faint image of the mandala has nestled deeply within my consciousness and it encapsulated a vision of spirituality that has grown within me for over the course of my lifetime. The mandala provided me with a visual symbol of the limitless capacity of the human spirit. In 2001, I was able to describe my vision of the mandala to dear artist friend who helped me to pull it from my subconscious and render it with watercolors. Then, as I scanned and digitized the image, the colors became more vivid as if they lived in a stained glass window backlit by the sun.

This mandala evokes the universal longing for inclusivity, equality, peace, wisdom and love that is the profound spiritual aspiration of all living beings. As I work with the mandala and share it with others, its teachings gradually are being revealed. May it help all beings to develop the fullness of their own spiritual potential.

APPENDIX B
"A MEDITATION PRACTICE TO HEAL THE CAUSES OF CHRONIC PAIN"

PERHAPS LIKE YOU, I have suffered the physical pains of injuries and the emotional pains of divorce and death of loved ones. I have found that Buddhism provided me with perspective on these and helped ameliorate the suffering, but my understanding and practice was not sufficient to heal them. I remember thinking . . . "Where was Buddhism when I most needed it?" It sounded a lot like others who would say, "Where was God when I needed Him?" I knew that there was something missing in my understanding and practice.

PHYSICAL PAIN & SUFFERING AS A SPIRITUAL GIFT

After years of study with Geshe Donyo (Khensur), Geshe Sopa, Geshe Lobsang Tenzin (Khensur) and others, I had developed a foundation for a well-rounded Buddhist practice. I also realized that I couldn't replicate their paths because the circumstances of our lives are so different. I concluded that it would take many years of personal practice and "making into my own" before I could actualize the kind of wisdom, equanimity, and compassion that they exemplified.

This was especially true when it came to healing my chronic back pain. The following story recounts how my effort to heal this pain drew from my understanding of Buddhist principles and my practice of Buddhist meditation.

In the late summer of 2006, I was presented with an opportunity to put all those years of study and meditation into practice. I was laid up in bed with another bout of the chronic back pain that had periodically stricken me for many years. This episode was especially challenging because it came just before a major weekend retreat I was about to lead at La Casa de Maria in Santa Barbara. My strategy, as it often had been, was to go to the pain doctor for a shot in the affected part of the spine. The orthopedic explanation was that a nerve was being impacted by swelling caused by a broken vertebrae from a ski accident 8 years earlier and a basketball injury way back in college. The shot of cortisone would lessen the swelling and therefore quell the pain.

I went to the doctor, and I was able to lead the program and it went very well. The following week, I drove down to Pasadena, California to attend a program led by the Dalai Lama. After sitting in a rather uncomfortable seat for two days, my excruciating pain returned and so back to the doctor I went. But this time, the injection did not stop the pain and I was told that the nerve would have to be cut. As I pondered my options, a couple of things happened. First, I recalled my mother's "incurable headaches" from a head-on auto crash caused by a drunk driver that sent her flying into the windshield of my father's car in the late 1960s. After she was advised by the doctors to have the nerves cut, she began learning Transcendental Meditation from the daughter of a close friend. And it worked! Her headaches from the car crash never returned.

The second thing that happened was that I became extremely self-critical at my attitude toward pain and suffering. This incident caused me to look at myself with a direct critical eye and say to myself: "You are a big phony! All these years you have been practicing meditation and you're still trying to give your pain away to a doctor. It is time you dealt with the psychological causes of your pain. It is time to connect the dots between your Buddhist meditation and your pain. How can you pretend to teach meditation if your practice hasn't alleviated the pain and suffering in your own back?" It was then that I developed a fierce resolve to deal with the causes of my chronic back pain through the application of meditation rather than medication.

Up to that point in my life, I had not expected meditation to have an immediate payoff, and had been sanguine with the promise of its "deferred benefit" in the next life. True, I had success using meditation to alleviate things like stress, cuts and burns and headaches. I felt that meditation increased my overall wisdom, compassion and equanimity. But when it came to back pain, I was not able to make significant progress. I reconciled myself to the opinion that some of life's pain and suffering were simply existential realities, that the karmic causes were so deep that I should not expect to be immediately healed.

As I lay there in pain, my friend Nancy Belle Coe lent me a book by Dr. Robert Sarno called *Healing Back Pain, The Mind Body Connection*. The book was a revelation to me for several reasons. First, it was written by a legitimate Orthopedic MD, who saw beyond the blinders of his own discipline. Second, it proposed that back pain was caused by a combination of psychological and physical issues. Third, it provided a bridge to my Buddhist meditation practice that might help me to heal both the physical and psychological causes of pain.

I developed a fierce resolution to create a meditative cure, and over the coming months I began writing a detailed journal chronicling my progress. Since the details of this meditative process require many pages and special verbal instruction, I will only provide a brief outline below. In doing so, I am using the three-stage technique for deep learning used in the Buddhist education system of Tibet. These are: (1) Learning, (2) Contemplation and (3) Meditation.

THE THEORY AND PRACTICE OF HEALING MEDITATION

First, here is an outline of the Buddhist-inspired principles I have learned from others and that I have refined in my own meditative experiments with pain and suffering. While these principles and processes have not been verified by medicine and neuroscience, I can attest for them based on my own experience as well as the testimonies of other experienced Buddhist colleagues and teachers. So please analyze them critically and adapt those elements that work for you.

1. Pain is inevitable. Suffering is optional. The severity of our suffering is proportional to the quality of our response to pain. We can alleviate our pain and suffering through understanding and practicing the shared principles of Buddhism, psychology, and medicine.

2. Pain in the body can result from physical injury. But this is not always the case. There are many reports of people with severe injuries who don't experience pain.

3. Old physical injuries, (like the damaged vertebrae in my back

from a skiing accident) are not sufficient causes of occasional, re-occurring pain. If they were, we would be in constant pain.

4. Physical pain can be caused by emotional unhappiness resulting from such things as economic stress, the death of a friend, the loss of a job, rejection by a parent, childhood trauma, verbal or physical abuse. This emotionally caused pain often appears to be located in the same place of an old injury or another type of physical anomaly. When pain occurs in the area of a previous injury, we mistakenly blame the pain on an old injury rather than an associated negative emotion.

5. Pain can be our greatest teacher for it can draw our attention to inner emotional issues that need to be acknowledged and healed.

6. From the Buddhist perspective, negative emotions are part of the karmic residue from this and previous lives. Karma is the internal law of cause and effect. The karmic seeds in our consciousness are planted by previous thoughts, words and actions. These seeds will bear their fruit in the future. Our negative emotions are karmic results from bad thoughts, words and actions. Negative emotions bear fruit in the form of pain and suffering. These negative emotions can be purified by meditations on wisdom and compassion.

7. We have a choice about how we respond to the onset of physical pain. If we respond to pain with fear, loathing and anger, the pain will only get worse and the healing will be slowed or stopped. A physical injury can heal more quickly if we don't overreact to the pain with anger or fear.

8. If we respond to pain with gratitude and curiosity we transform the pain from an enemy into an ally. Therefore, at the onset of pain it helps to say "thank you!" rather than "damn you!" Gratitude changes the emotional and physiological response to the pain from reactive to proactive. Gratitude neutralizes the detrimental power of pain over our emotions and the body's healing response.

9. The techniques of meditation and visualization can help us to stop the pain, cure the causes of the pain, and eliminate the suffering that emerges from pain.

CONTEMPLATION
Before we engage in the actual meditation, we review these

principles and practices through deep contemplation.

1. Relax quietly in a comfortable position. Breath gently in and out and imagine healing energy of subtle breath circulating throughout your whole body

2. Remind yourself that pain is a great teacher. It is forcing you to deal with your "inner emotional issues." If you don't deal with these, you will have to endure their debilitating effects forever. Renew your commitment to heal the emotional causes rather than just the physical pain through drugs and physical therapy.

3. Commit yourself to 'opening up to' and healing the emotional wounds of your lifetime that have been stored in your unconscious mind.

4. Realize that the pain does not solely emanate from the place where you feel it. Rather, pain it is a sensation caused by a myriad of interrelated psychological, neurological, emotional and physiological issues.

5. Say "thank you!" to the pain. Vow that whenever the pain reoccurs in the future that your first response will be gratitude.

6. Look at the pain with curiosity rather than dread. Realize that pain is not an independent force that has power to make you suffer. Rather, pain is an impermanent and interdependent phenomena and empty of its own independent existence. Pain is the result of many interrelated physical and mental factors. Pain is not solely caused by an injury or an intrusion on the nerve fibers. If this were the case, you would always be in pain.

7. Engage in the following contemplative visualization as part of the process to stop the pain and suffering. (Note: This is a visualization exercise, not scientific explanation).

(a) Imagine that your conscious mind and unconscious minds are both surrounded by a translucent, semi-permeable membrane. These imagined spheres that separate the conscious and the unconscious minds are like the ultra-thin membranes surrounding the alveoli in your lungs through which oxygen and carbon dioxide are transferred into the red blood cells. The negative emotions can flow from the unconscious to the conscious mind through these semi-permeable membranes.

(b) Visualize the brainstem at the base of your skull as the control center of autonomic systems of the body. This is the connection point of the body's nerves that travel up the spine to the brain. Imagine that it is in the brain stem that the autonomic nervous system regulates the flow of blood, other chemical substances and electrical impulses throughout the body. It regulates these systems in response to the physical stimuli of the body, the conceptual stimuli of the conscious mind, and the hidden emotional stimuli within the unconscious mind.

(c) Visualize that the brainstem and autonomic system are the transfer points for negative emotions between the conscious and unconscious mind. Imagine that negative emotions stored in the unconscious mind filter through the conduit of the brainstem. The autonomic system then responds to these emotions by altering the physiological state within the body.

(8) The autonomic system cannot directly communicate with the thoughts, concepts, and sensory awareness of the conscious mind. Rather, it communicates indirectly with the conscious mind by altering the physiological states in your body. For example, the autonomic system can shunt blood vessels to the muscles and nerves in your back that might have been previously injured. This lack of blood flow and oxygen deprivation to the muscle causes the nerves in that part of the body to send a distress signal to the brain which is interpreted as pain that is the result of a muscle injury. That ensuing feeling of pain is caused by the autonomic system responding to the presence of a negative emotion by shunting blood flow.

(9) The immediate cause of the pain, therefore, is not an injured muscle. Rather, the sensation of pain is caused by the combination of these interdependent factors: (a) a negative emotion emerging from the unconscious mind, (b) the existence of a formerly injured muscle, (c) the shunting of blood by the autonomic system to that muscle, (d) an electrical impulse from a nerve in the muscle to the brain, (e) the perception and interpretation of that impulse by the conscious mind and (f) an incorrect interpretation that the sole cause of the pain is an injury to the muscle.

(10) The autonomic system will continue to cause pain in the area of muscle until the conscious mind begins to deal with the

underlying emotional causes of the pain. When this happens, the conscious mind should say to the unconscious mind, "Thank you! I am dealing with the causes now. You no longer a need to cause this pain."

(11) At first, the conscious mind mistakenly thinks that this pain is originating in the back and assumes that it is caused by a back injury. Therefore it seeks relief through drugs and physical therapy rather than meditation.

(12) However, the conscious mind can change its first response and choose how to respond to the sensation of pain. A wise response would be to consider the possible emotional causes along with the physical causes.

MEDITATION

The following is a meditation to help heal the causes and suffering from pain. These steps coincide with the seven step process of InterSpiritual Meditation. Please analyze and assess these and adapt them to your own meditative process.

(1) MOTIVATION – THE FIERCE RESOLVE TO BECOME HEALTHY AND HAPPY

Develop a fierce resolve to become healthy and happy and to heal the causes of your pain. Engage in preliminary breathing techniques to calm the overall physical effects of the pain. Breathe gently into your heart-center when you feel the pain beginning to return. Realize that without mindful breathing the pain would engulf and control you. To control the pain, you need to step back, breath easily and learn the lessons that your autonomic system (and the pain) is trying to teach you.

(2) GRATITUDE

Sincerely thank your pain for drawing your attention to the hidden negative emotions buried in your unconscious mind. By thanking the pain, you will recondition your first automatic response to pain into one of gratitude rather than one of anger and resentment. In this way, the experience of pain can become something positive rather than something negative.

(3) TRANSFORMATION

Consider your pain a transformative opportunity for actualizing your highest possible state of being. It points you to internal psychological and physiological issues that need healing. It is an ally and a teacher. It can spur you to equanimous wisdom and boundless compassion. As human beings, pain is inevitable; but suffering is not. So use it to advance your highest aspirations.

(4) LOVE, FORGIVENESS AND COMPASSION FOR YOURSELF AND OTHERS

Here, you renew your compassionate vow to help others. This begins by forgiving yourself and others for their part in the negative emotion. Remind yourself that this meditation is not just a narcissistic exercise, but rather an opportunity to heal your pain and suffering so that you can help others do the same. Remind yourself that love, forgiveness and compassion for others is a necessary condition in one's own self-healing process.

(5) FOCUS ON MINDFUL BREATHING

Begin by breathing gently, inhaling through the nose and exhaling through the nose or mouth. Once you develop a comfortable and calm rhythm, allow your conscious awareness to ride the breath deep into the lungs. As you do this, feel your conscious awareness recede from your senses and gather in the center of your chest. Activate your capacity to observe any distractions that might draw your attention away from your breathing.

(6) MEDITATION

The following is a Buddhist inspired meditation technique to transform the pain into an opportunity for spiritual growth, healing and eliminating pain and suffering.

(a) All phenomena are interdependent, impermanent, empty of inherent existence. Pain is a phenomena. Therefore pain is also interdependent, impermanent, and empty.

(b) "Breath down" your conscious awareness and imagine that it rests at the intersection of the spheres of the conscious and unconscious minds. As your conscious awareness hovers there, it calmly watches for the presence of a negative emotion that might be nearing the conduit of the brain stem. Your conscious awareness is accompanied by several meditative attributes: (1) Wisdom of the impermanence, interdependence and emptiness of any negative emotion that appears. (2) Forgiveness for yourself and others connected with any negative emotion that appears. (3) Compassionate love for the that emotion and anyone connected to it. When a negative emotion appears, bathe it in these attributes and witness the release of the negative energy from these emotions.

(c) Apply this same meditative process to all the unseen negative emotions in your unconscious mind. Imagine how they are all bathed in your wisdom, forgiveness and compassion. In this way, our meditative process will healing and dissolve any negative emotion before it enters the brain stem and autonomic system. When we do this, the cause of the pain can be healed and eliminated. Therefore, the healing process doesn't need to be focused on each specific negative emotion. Rather, the waves of this healing process spread throughout the unconscious mind to become a healing elixir for a whole class of negative emotions whether or not they are directly observed.

(7) DEDICATION

We end the session of healing meditation with a dedication to help others to transform their experience of pain into an opportunity for wisdom, forgiveness, love, and healing. We vow to use this meditation whenever we begin to feel the onset of pain. We dedicate ourselves to maintaining this perspective for the benefit of others.

FOLLOW-UP PRACTICES

The purpose of this meditation is to recondition our conscious mind to alter its normal habitual response to pain and to focus on healing the underlying emotional causes of pain. I have found that in order for this practice to work, it must become part of our everyday lives. Therefore, please consider the following statements of commitment:

1. I commit to practice this meditation daily as needed so that I might alleviate my pain and heal the causes of pain and suffering. I will be fierce in my practice knowing that it will require powerful intention and perseverance to achieve these goals.

2. I commit to saying "thank you" whenever I begin to feel the onset of pain. I will be grateful to pain for drawing my attention to the innermost emotional causes of pain. I

commit myself to doing this meditation at the very first signs of pain because the earlier I catch the pain the better I will become at alleviating it and curing its causes.

3. When I experience pain, I will meditate on the emotional causes of the pain and bath these with healing elixirs of love, forgiveness and the wisdom of interdependence, impermanence and emptiness.

4. I will perfect this meditation so that I might be an example for others who wish to eliminate their pain and suffering.

A Personal Note

I developed this Buddhist-inspired meditation because I saw how my own chronic pattern of pain would continue to repeat itself over and over until my conscious mind began to deal directly with all the unresolved emotional issues residing in the unconscious mind. I found that through many repetitions of this meditation, I was able to break the chronic pattern of pain in my back that I had experienced for over thirty years. But I still feel occasional pain in other parts of my body. So I consider myself lucky to have so many teachers and so many opportunities for gratitude! I continue to persist when new pains emerge knowing that this meditation helps me to maintain a state of equanimity, to alleviate the pain, heal the causes of suffering and to deepen my spiritual practice. I don't expect this practice to stop all the normal pains of aging; but it does relieve the suffering I used to experience and it helps me to help others do the same.

Dr. Edward W. Bastian holds a Ph.D. in Buddhist Studies and is the founder and president of the Spiritual Paths Foundation. His current writing and teaching is the product of over forty years of research and study, especially in the last decades with over fifty esteemed teachers of Buddhism, Christianity, Hinduism, Islam, Judaism, Taoism, and Native American traditions. He is the award winning co-author of *Living Fully Dying Well* (2009), author of *InterSpiritual Meditation* (2010), and producer of various documentaries on religion for the BBC and PBS.

Bastian is the former co-director of the Forum on BioDiversity for the Smithsonian and National Academy of Sciences, teacher of Buddhism and world religions at the Smithsonian, an Internet entrepreneur and translator of Buddhist scriptures from Tibetan into English. He is also an Adjunct Professor at Antioch University in Santa Barbara where he is teaching courses on Buddhism and Mindfulness Meditation. Bastian also teaches on-line courses as well as seminars and retreats at such organizations as One Spirit Interfaith, Chaplaincy Institute, CIIS, Sacred Art of Living and Dying, Interspiritual Centre of Vancouver, Cascadia Center, Esalen Institute, Omega Institute, Hollyhock Retreat Center, Garrison Institute and La Casa de Maria.

He is the Co-President of the Interfaith Initiative of Santa Barbara, co-founder of ECOFaith Santa Barbara and Trustee of the United Religions Initiative Global Council.

49009110R00135

Made in the USA
Middletown, DE
02 October 2017